Bryn Mawr Greek Commentaries

The Shorter Homeric Hymns

Lee T. Pearcy

Thomas Library, Bryn Mawr College

Bryn Mawr, Pennsylvania

Copyright ©1989 by **Bryn Mawr Commentarie**

Manufactured in the United States of America
ISBN 0-929524-62-4
Printed and distributed by

Bryn Mawr Commentaries
Thomas Library
Bryn Mawr College
Bryn Mawr, PA 19010

SERIES PREFACE

These lexical and grammatical notes are meant not as a full-scale commentary but as a clear and concise aid to the beginning student. The editors have been told to resist their critical impulses and to say only what will help the student read the text. Our commentaries, then, are the beginning of the interpretative process, not the end. We expect that the student will know the basic Attic declensions and conjugations, basic grammar (the common functions of cases and moods; the common types of clauses and conditions), and how to use a dictionary. In general we have tried to avoid duplication of material easily extractable from the lexicon; but we have included help with odd verb forms, and, recognizing that endless page-flipping can be counter-productive, we have provided the occasional bonus of assistance with uncommon vocabulary.

The commentaries are based on the Oxford Classical Text unless otherwise noted. Oxford University Press has kindly allowed us to print its edition of the Greek text in cases where we thought it would be particularly beneficial to the student. Production of these texts has been made possible by a generous grant from the Division of Educational Programs, the National Endowment for the Humanities.

>Richard Hamilton, General Editor
>Gregory W. Dickerson, Associate Editor
>Gilbert P. Rose, Associate Editor
>
>Bryn Mawr Greek Commentaries

VOLUME PREFACE

In addition to the four long hymns to Demeter, Delian and Pythian Apollo, Hermes, and Aphrodite, the collection which has come down from antiquity under the name Homeric Hymns contains 28 other complete hymns as well as a fragment of a long hymn to Dionysus and an epigram, Εἰς Ξένους. It is not possible to say when any single hymn was composed. Some, like the Hymn to Aphrodite (VI), may be as early as the seventh century B.C. The Hymn to Ares (VIII), on the other hand, seems to show the influence of Neoplatonism and may be as late as the fifth century A.D.

The collection itself may not have been put together until late antiquity. The ancient commentaries, or scholia, on Homer do not quote the hymns at many points where they might have. This omission indicates that the Alexandrian scholars of the third and second centuries B.C., whose work lies behind the Homeric scholia, did not study the hymns.

What, then, are the hymns? Thucydides (III.104) calls the long Hymn to Apollo a προοίμιον or prelude, and most of the shorter hymns could have been used as preludes to recitations of epic poetry by rhapsodes. Long and short hymns alike usually end with a formula of transition to another song. But like a musical prelude, the προοίμιον could have an independent existence, and some of the longer hymns are as long as a book of the Odyssey, perhaps too long to be used as true preludes. Likewise the hymn, although fundamentally an invocation of a god and often connected with some particular cult or sanctuary, soon became as much a literary as a devotional genre. The students for whom this series is intended will, I hope, find these shorter Homeric Hymns valuable as compact introductions to the language of epic and the gods of Greece.

        Lee T. Pearcy
        Merion, Pennsylvania
        September 1, 1987

THE LANGUAGE OF THE HYMNS

The Homeric Hymns, like the Iliad and the Odyssey, were composed in an artificial dialect made up of elements taken from Greek spoken at different times in different parts of the Hellenic world. This epic language is fundamentally Ionic and Aeolic, with a few neologisms and forms from other dialects. No one ever spoke the language of Homer, any more than the language of Spenser or Milton. The epic dialect developed on the lips of generations of bards as a medium for oral composition of heroic poems. An oral poet built his verse out of formulae, fixed phrases appropriate to each situation in the epic narrative and to each metrical position in the hexameter line. The variety of forms available in the epic dialect increased the flexibility and efficiency of the formulaic system, and the artificiality of the medium increased the universality of the message. Since epic Greek was the language of no particular branch of the Hellenes, Homeric poetry could belong to them all.

The following are the chief morphological differences, as seen in the shorter Homeric Hymns, between epic and Attic Greek. For a more detailed account, see W. B. Stanford, The Odyssey of Homer (London, 1965), lii-lxxxvi, and D. B. Monro, Grammar of the Homeric Dialect (Oxford, 1891).

I. Vowels
1. Epic has η for Attic long α: νεηνίη (VII.3) for νεανίᾳ.
2. Epic has considerable variation in the quantity of vowels and between long vowels and diphthongs:
Διώνυσον VII.1, Διόνυσος VII.56,
νεῶν (ships) XXXIII.7, νηῶν XXXIII.8.
Diphthongs are sometimes pronounced as two syllables: εὔτυκτον VI.7, ἐϋπλοκάμῳ XIX.34, ἠΰκομον XIII.1.
3. Vowel combinations contracted in Attic are left uncontracted in epic:
ἥν περ καλέουσι Θυώνην I.21.
II. Consonants
1. Epic shows traces of the digamma, a labial spirant pronounced like w and written ϝ. Many examples of hiatus, the juxtaposition of one word ending with a vowel with another

beginning with a vowel, can be explained by the presence of an unwritten digamma:
περὶ δ' ἄμβροτα (ϝ)εἵματα (ϝ)έσσαν VI.6.
   2. Epic frequently omits the aspirate where Attic has it (S 9D), writing e.g. ἠέλιος for ἥλιος and ἐπίημι for ἐφίημι.
III. Nouns and adjectives
   1. Second declension nouns and adjectives show a gen. sg. in -οιο as well as -ου:
ἀμβρόσιον πίνοντες ὕδωρ <u>ξανθοῦ ποταμοῖο</u> XXXIV.4.
   2. First and second declension nouns and adjectives show a dat. pl. in -ῃσι (and -ῃς) or -οισι well as -αις and -οις:
<u>λιγυρῇσιν</u> ἀγαλλόμενος φρένα <u>μολπαῖς</u> XIX.24,
ὃς φαίνει θνητοῖσι καὶ ἀθανάτοισι <u>θεοῖσιν</u> XXXI.8,
ὅ γ' ἅπασι <u>θεοῖς</u> θοὸς ἄγγελός ἐστι XIX.29.
   3. Third declension nouns show a dat. pl. in -εσσι or -σσι:
ὅδε δ' αὖτ' <u>ἄνδρεσσι</u> μελήσει VII.27.
IV. Pronouns
   1. The personal pronouns show a variety of forms. The following variants are found in the shorter hymns:
ἐγών 1st pers. sg. nom.
ἄμμι 1st pers. pl. dat.
σεῖο, σέο, σεῦ, σέθεν 2nd pers. sg. gen.
ὑμέων pers. pl. gen.
τοι (once) 2nd pers. sg. dat.
οἱ 3rd pers. sg. dat.
σφιν 3rd pers. pl. dat.
μιν 3rd pers. sg. acc.
   2. ὁ, ἡ, τό is used as a weak demonstrative pronoun (S 1099):
<u>τὴν</u> δὲ χρυσάμπυκες Ὧραι / δέξαντ' VI.5-6.
V. Verbs
   1. The augment is frequently omitted (S 438c):
εἰμὶ δ' ἐγὼ Διόνυσος ἐρίβρομος ὃν <u>τέκε</u> μήτηρ VII.56.
   2. Many verbs compounded with prepositional prefixes (e.g. περί, κατά, κ.τ.λ.) appear to have these prefixes separated from the base verb:
δέξαντ' ἀσπασίως, <u>περὶ</u> δ' ἄμβροτα εἵματα <u>ἕσσαν</u> VI.6.
These apparently detachable prefixes are in fact "preposition-adverbs" (S 1638), which in epic have not yet become specialized as prefixes to verbs (e.g. περιέννυμι) or as prepositions.
   3. Infinitives show the endings -μεν and -μεναι for -ειν and -ναι. The accent falls on the syllable preceding the ending (S 469D):
ἐπιβαινέμεν = ἐπιβαίνειν VIII.15,
ἔμεναι = εἶναι XXII.5.

METRICAL NOTE

The Homeric Hymns are composed in dactylic hexameter, which is the normal meter of Greek and Latin epic poetry. Each line (hexameter) has six measures (= metra) or feet, which may be either dactyls (diagrammed - υ υ, where - is a long syllable and υ a short one) or spondees (diagrammed - -). The sixth (last) foot is always a spondee or a trochee (- υ). The first five are either spondees or dactyls, with dactyls predominating, especially in the fifth foot, which is spondaic about one out of 20 times in the Iliad and Odyssey. Line 9 of Hymn VI is such a "spondaic" verse. The first verse of Hymn VI is analyzed or "scanned" as follows:

αἰδοίην χρυσοστέφανον καλὴν Ἀφροδίτην
- -| - -| - υ υ| - -| - υ υ| - - |

A syllable is long if it contains (a) a long vowel or diphthong or (b) a short vowel followed by two consonants. The vowel of a syllable lengthened by two following consonants is said to be long "by position." One or both consonants may belong to the beginning of the following word. ζ, ξ, and ψ count as double consonants. Digamma ("Language of Hymns" II.1) may be one of the two consonants.

 The combination of a mute consonant (π, τ, κ, β, δ, γ, φ, θ, and χ) followed by a liquid consonant (λ or ρ) in the same word need not lengthen the preceding syllable, as can be seen in the first syllable of Ἀφροδίτην above.

 A syllable is short if it contains a short vowel and is not lengthened by the double consonant rule (b). The Greek vowels ε and o are always short; η and ω are always long; α, ι, and υ may be long or short by nature, and their natural quantities in the root of any given word are noted in the lexicon.

 In epic, a long vowel or diphthong is regularly but not always shortened in pronunciation if it ends a word and is directly followed by a word which begins with a vowel. This shortening, called "epic correption," can be seen in line 20 of Hymn VI, φέρεσθαι ἐμήν, scanned υ - υ υ -.

Word-ending <u>within</u> a foot is called "caesura." Word-ending coinciding with the <u>end</u> of a foot is called "diaeresis." The epic dactylic hexameter virtually always has a caesura within the third foot and commonly a diaeresis at the end of the fourth. These two positions frequently mark an important pause in a sentence or a break between sentences, but significant word-breaks may, and frequently do, occur elsewhere in the verse.

For a more detailed account of the structure of Homeric verse, see G. S. Kirk, ed., <u>The Iliad: A Commentary</u>, vol. 1 (Cambridge, 1985), 17-37.

I
To Dionysus (fragments)

οἱ μὲν γὰρ Δρακάνῳ σ', οἱ δ' Ἰκάρῳ ἠνεμοέσσῃ 1
φάσ', οἱ δ' ἐν Νάξῳ, δῖον γένος εἰραφιῶτα,
οἱ δέ σ' ἐπ' Ἀλφειῷ ποταμῷ βαθυδινήεντι
κυσαμένην Σεμέλην τεκέειν Διὶ τερπικεραύνῳ,
ἄλλοι δ' ἐν Θήβῃσιν ἄναξ σε λέγουσι γενέσθαι 5
ψευδόμενοι· σὲ δ' ἔτικτε πατὴρ ἀνδρῶν τε θεῶν τε
πολλὸν ἀπ' ἀνθρώπων κρύπτων λευκώλενον Ἥρην.
ἔστι δέ τις Νύσῃ ὕπατον ὄρος ἀνθέον ὕλῃ
τηλοῦ Φοινίκης σχεδὸν Αἰγύπτοιο ῥοάων

καί οἱ ἀναστήσουσιν ἀγάλματα πόλλ' ἐνὶ νηοῖς. 10
ὡς δὲ τάμεν τρία, σοὶ πάντως τριετηρίσιν αἰεὶ
ἄνθρωποι ῥέξουσι τεληέσσας ἑκατόμβας.
ἦ καὶ κυανέῃσιν ἐπ' ὀφρύσι νεῦσε Κρονίων·
ἀμβρόσιαι δ' ἄρα χαῖται ἐπερρώσαντο ἄνακτος
κρατὸς ἀπ' ἀθανάτοιο, μέγαν δ' ἐλέλιξεν Ὄλυμπον. 15
ὣς εἰπὼν ἐκέλευσε καρήατι μητίετα Ζεύς.
ἵληθ' εἰραφιῶτα γυναιμανές· οἱ δέ σ' ἀοιδοὶ
ᾄδομεν ἀρχόμενοι λήγοντές τ', οὐδέ πῃ ἔστι
σεῖ' ἐπιληθομένῳ ἱερῆς μεμνῆσθαι ἀοιδῆς.
καὶ σὺ μὲν οὕτω χαῖρε Διώνυσ' εἰραφιῶτα, 20
σὺν μητρὶ Σεμέλῃ ἥν περ καλέουσι Θυώνην.

VI
To Aphrodite

Αἰδοίην χρυσοστέφανον καλὴν Ἀφροδίτην 1
ᾄσομαι, ἣ πάσης Κύπρου κρήδεμνα λέλογχεν
εἰναλίης, ὅθι μιν Ζεφύρου μένος ὑγρὸν ἀέντος
ἤνεικεν κατὰ κῦμα πολυφλοίσβοιο θαλάσσης
ἀφρῷ ἔνι μαλακῷ· τὴν δὲ χρυσάμπυκες Ὧραι 5
δέξαντ' ἀσπασίως, περὶ δ' ἄμβροτα εἵματα ἕσσαν,
κρατὶ δ' ἐπ' ἀθανάτῳ στεφάνην εὔτυκτον ἔθηκαν
καλὴν χρυσείην, ἐν δὲ τρητοῖσι λοβοῖσιν
ἄνθεμ' ὀρειχάλκου χρυσοῖό τε τιμήεντος,
δειρῇ δ' ἀμφ' ἁπαλῇ καὶ στήθεσιν ἀργυφέοισιν 10
ὅρμοισι χρυσέοισιν ἐκόσμεον οἷσί περ αὐταὶ
Ὧραι κοσμείσθην χρυσάμπυκες ὁππότ' ἴοιεν
ἐς χορὸν ἱμερόεντα θεῶν καὶ δώματα πατρός.

αὐτὰρ ἐπεὶ δὴ πάντα περὶ χροῒ κόσμον ἔθηκαν
ἦγον ἐς ἀθανάτους· οἱ δ' ἠσπάζοντο ἰδόντες 15
χερσί τ' ἐδεξιόωντο καὶ ἠρήσαντο ἕκαστος
εἶναι κουριδίην ἄλοχον καὶ οἴκαδ' ἄγεσθαι,
εἶδος θαυμάζοντες ἰοστεφάνου Κυθερείης.
Χαῖρ' ἑλικοβλέφαρε γλυκυμείλιχε, δὸς δ' ἐν ἀγῶνι
νίκην τῷδε φέρεσθαι, ἐμὴν δ' ἔντυνον ἀοιδήν. 20
αὐτὰρ ἐγὼ καὶ σεῖο καὶ ἄλλης μνήσομ' ἀοιδῆς.

VII
To Dionysus

Ἀμφὶ Διώνυσον Σεμέλης ἐρικυδέος υἱὸν 1
μνήσομαι, ὡς ἐφάνη παρὰ θῖν' ἁλὸς ἀτρυγέτοιο
ἀκτῇ ἐπὶ προβλῆτι νεηνίῃ ἀνδρὶ ἐοικὼς
πρωθήβῃ· καλαὶ δὲ περισσείοντο ἔθειραι
κυάνεαι, φᾶρος δὲ περὶ στιβαροῖς ἔχεν ὤμοις 5
πορφύρεον· τάχα δ' ἄνδρες ἐϋσσέλμου ἀπὸ νηὸς
ληϊσταὶ προγένοντο θοῶς ἐπὶ οἴνοπα πόντον
Τυρσηνοί· τοὺς δ' ἦγε κακὸς μόρος· οἱ δὲ ἰδόντες
νεῦσαν ἐς ἀλλήλους, τάχα δ' ἔκθορον, αἶψα δ' ἑλόντες
εἷσαν ἐπὶ σφετέρης νηὸς κεχαρημένοι ἦτορ. 10
υἱὸν γάρ μιν ἔφαντο διοτρεφέων βασιλήων
εἶναι, καὶ δεσμοῖς ἔθελον δεῖν ἀργαλέοισι.
τὸν δ' οὐκ ἴσχανε δεσμά, λύγοι δ' ἀπὸ τηλόσ' ἔπιπτον
χειρῶν ἠδὲ ποδῶν· ὁ δὲ μειδιάων ἐκάθητο
ὄμμασι κυανέοισι, κυβερνήτης δὲ νοήσας 15
αὐτίκα οἷς ἑτάροισιν ἐκέκλετο φώνησέν τε·
Δαιμόνιοι τίνα τόνδε θεὸν δεσμεύεθ' ἑλόντες
καρτερόν; οὐδὲ φέρειν δύναταί μιν νηῦς ἐυεργής.
ἦ γὰρ Ζεὺς ὅδε γ' ἐστὶν ἢ ἀργυρότοξος Ἀπόλλων
ἠὲ Ποσειδάων· ἐπεὶ οὐ θνητοῖσι βροτοῖσιν 20
εἴκελος, ἀλλὰ θεοῖς οἳ Ὀλύμπια δώματ' ἔχουσιν.
ἀλλ' ἄγετ' αὐτὸν ἀφῶμεν ἐπ' ἠπείροιο μελαίνης
αὐτίκα, μηδ' ἐπὶ χεῖρας ἰάλλετε μή τι χολωθεὶς
ὄρσῃ ἀργαλέους τ' ἀνέμους καὶ λαίλαπα πολλήν.
Ὣς φάτο· τὸν δ' ἀρχὸς στυγερῷ ἠνίπαπε μύθῳ· 25
δαιμόνι' οὖρον ὅρα, ἅμα δ' ἱστίον ἕλκεο νηὸς
σύμπανθ' ὅπλα λαβών· ὅδε δ' αὖτ' ἄνδρεσσι μελήσει.
ἔλπομαι ἢ Αἴγυπτον ἀφίξεται ἢ ὅ γε Κύπρον
ἢ ἐς Ὑπερβορέους ἢ ἑκαστέρω· ἐς δὲ τελευτὴν
ἔκ ποτ' ἐρεῖ αὐτοῦ τε φίλους καὶ κτήματα πάντα 30

οὕς τε κασιγνήτους, ἐπεὶ ἡμῖν ἔμβαλε δαίμων.
Ὣς εἰπὼν ἱστόν τε καὶ ἱστίον ἕλκετο νηός.
ἔμπνευσεν δ' ἄνεμος μέσον ἱστίον, ἀμφὶ δ' ἄρ' ὅπλα
καττάνυσαν· τάχα δέ σφιν ἐφαίνετο θαυματὰ ἔργα.
οἶνος μὲν πρώτιστα θοὴν ἀνὰ νῆα μέλαιναν 35
ἡδύποτος κελάρυζ' εὐώδης, ὤρνυτο δ' ὀδμὴ
ἀμβροσίη· ναύτας δὲ τάφος λάβε πάντας ἰδόντας.
αὐτίκα δ' ἀκρότατον παρὰ ἱστίον ἐξετανύσθη
ἄμπελος ἔνθα καὶ ἔνθα, κατεκρημνῶντο δὲ πολλοὶ
βότρυες· ἀμφ' ἱστὸν δὲ μέλας εἱλίσσετο κισσὸς 40
ἄνθεσι τηλεθάων, χαρίεις δ' ἐπὶ καρπὸς ὀρώρει·
πάντες δὲ σκαλμοὶ στεφάνους ἔχον· οἱ δὲ ἰδόντες
νῆ' ἤδη τότ' ἔπειτα κυβερνήτην ἐκέλευον
γῇ πελάαν· ὁ δ' ἄρα σφι λέων γένετ' ἔνδοθι νηὸς
δεινὸς ἐπ' ἀκροτάτης, μέγα δ' ἔβραχεν, ἐν δ' ἄρα μέσσῃ 45
ἄρκτον ἐποίησεν λασιαύχενα σήματα φαίνων·
ἂν δ' ἔστη μεμαυῖα, λέων δ' ἐπὶ σέλματος ἄκρου
δεινὸν ὑπόδρα ἰδών· οἱ δ' εἰς πρύμνην ἐφόβηθεν,
ἀμφὶ κυβερνήτην δὲ σαόφρονα θυμὸν ἔχοντα
ἔσταν ἄρ' ἐκπληγέντες· ὁ δ' ἐξαπίνης ἐπορούσας 50
ἀρχὸν ἕλ', οἱ δὲ θύραζε κακὸν μόρον ἐξαλύοντες
πάντες ὁμῶς πήδησαν ἐπεὶ ἴδον εἰς ἅλα δῖαν,
δελφῖνες δ' ἐγένοντο· κυβερνήτην δ' ἐλεήσας
ἔσχεθε καί μιν ἔθηκε πανόλβιον εἶπέ τε μῦθον·
Θάρσει † δῖ' ἑκάτωρ τῷ ἐμῷ κεχαρισμένε θυμῷ· 55
εἰμὶ δ' ἐγὼ Διόνυσος ἐρίβρομος ὃν τέκε μήτηρ
Καδμηῒς Σεμέλη Διὸς ἐν φιλότητι μιγεῖσα.
Χαῖρε τέκος Σεμέλης εὐώπιδος· οὐδέ πῃ ἔστι
σεῖό γε ληθόμενον γλυκερὴν κοσμῆσαι ἀοιδήν.

VIII
To Ares

Ἆρες ὑπερμενέτα, βρισάρματε, χρυσεοπήληξ, 1
ὀβριμόθυμε, φέρασπι, πολισσόε, χαλκοκορυστά,
καρτερόχειρ, ἀμόγητε, δορυσθενές, ἕρκος Ὀλύμπου,
Νίκης εὐπολέμοιο πάτερ, συναρωγὲ Θέμιστος,
ἀντιβίοισι τύραννε, δικαιοτάτων ἀγὲ φωτῶν, 5
ἠνορέης σκηπτοῦχε, πυραυγέα κύκλον ἑλίσσων
αἰθέρος ἑπταπόροις ἐνὶ τείρεσιν ἔνθα σε πῶλοι
ζαφλεγέες τριτάτης ὑπὲρ ἄντυγος αἰὲν ἔχουσι·
κλῦθι βροτῶν ἐπίκουρε, δοτὴρ εὐθαλέος ἥβης,

πρηΰ καταστίλβων σέλας ὑψόθεν ἐς βιότητα 10
ἡμετέρην καὶ κάρτος ἀρήϊον, ὥς κε δυναίμην
σεύασθαι κακότητα πικρὴν ἀπ' ἐμοῖο καρήνου,
καὶ ψυχῆς ἀπατηλὸν ὑπογνάμψαι φρεσὶν ὁρμὴν
θυμοῦ τ' αὖ μένος ὀξὺ κατισχέμεν ὅς μ' ἐρέθῃσι
φυλόπιδος κρυερῆς ἐπιβαινέμεν· ἀλλὰ σὺ θάρσος 15
δὸς μάκαρ, εἰρήνης τε μένειν ἐν ἀπήμοσι θεσμοῖς
δυσμενέων προφυγόντα μόθον κῆράς τε βιαίους.

IX
To Artemis

Ἄρτεμιν ὕμνει Μοῦσα κασιγνήτην Ἑκάτοιο, 1
παρθένον ἰοχέαιραν, ὁμότροφον Ἀπόλλωνος,
ἥ θ' ἵππους ἄρσασα βαθυσχοίνοιο Μέλητος
ῥίμφα διὰ Σμύρνης παγχρύσεον ἅρμα διώκει
ἐς Κλάρον ἀμπελόεσσαν, ὅθ' ἀργυρότοξος Ἀπόλλων 5
ἧσται μιμνάζων ἑκατηβόλον ἰοχέαιραν.
Καὶ σὺ μὲν οὕτω χαῖρε θεαί θ' ἅμα πᾶσαι ἀοιδῇ·
αὐτὰρ ἐγώ σε πρῶτα καὶ ἐκ σέθεν ἄρχομ' ἀείδειν,
σεῦ δ' ἐγὼ ἀρξάμενος μεταβήσομαι ἄλλον ἐς ὕμνον.

X
To Aphrodite

Κυπρογενῆ Κυθέρειαν ἀείσομαι ἥ τε βροτοῖσι 1
μείλιχα δῶρα δίδωσιν, ἐφ' ἱμερτῷ δὲ προσώπῳ
αἰεὶ μειδιάει καὶ ἐφ' ἱμερτὸν θέει ἄνθος.
Χαῖρε θεὰ Σαλαμῖνος ἐϋκτιμένης μεδέουσα
εἰναλίης τε Κύπρου· δὸς δ' ἱμερόεσσαν ἀοιδήν. 5
αὐτὰρ ἐγὼ καὶ σεῖο καὶ ἄλλης μνήσομ' ἀοιδῆς.

XI
To Athena

Παλλάδ' Ἀθηναίην ἐρυσίπτολιν ἄρχομ' ἀείδειν 1
δεινήν, ᾗ σὺν Ἄρηϊ μέλει πολεμήϊα ἔργα
περθόμεναί τε πόληες ἀϋτή τε πτόλεμοί τε,
καί τ' ἐρρύσατο λαὸν ἰόντα τε νισόμενόν τε.
Χαῖρε θεά, δὸς δ' ἄμμι τύχην εὐδαιμονίην τε. 5

XII
To Hera

Ἥρην ἀείδω χρυσόθρονον ἣν τέκε Ῥείη, 1
ἀθανάτην βασίλειαν ὑπείροχον εἶδος ἔχουσαν
Ζηνὸς ἐριγδούποιο κασιγνήτην ἄλοχόν τε
κυδρήν, ἣν πάντες μάκαρες κατὰ μακρὸν Ὄλυμπον
ἁζόμενοι τίουσιν ὁμῶς Διὶ τερπικεραύνῳ. 5

XIII
To Demeter

Δήμητρ' ἠΰκομον σεμνὴν θεὰν ἄρχομ' ἀείδειν, 1
αὐτὴν καὶ κούρην, περικαλλέα Περσεφόνειαν.
Χαῖρε θεὰ καὶ τήνδε σάου πόλιν, ἄρχε δ' ἀοιδῆς.

XIV
To the Mother of the Gods

Μητέρα μοι πάντων τε θεῶν πάντων τ' ἀνθρώπων 1
ὕμνει Μοῦσα λίγεια Διὸς θυγάτηρ μεγάλοιο,
ᾗ κροτάλων τυπάνων τ' ἰαχὴ σύν τε βρόμος αὐλῶν
εὔαδεν, ἠδὲ λύκων κλαγγὴ χαροπῶν τε λεόντων,
οὔρεά τ' ἠχήεντα καὶ ὑλήεντες ἔναυλοι. 5
Καὶ σὺ μὲν οὕτω χαῖρε θεαί θ' ἅμα πᾶσαι ἀοιδῇ.

XV
To Lion-hearted Heracles

Ἡρακλέα Διὸς υἱὸν ἀείσομαι, ὃν μέγ' ἄριστον 1
γείνατ' ἐπιχθονίων Θήβης ἔνι καλλιχόροισιν
Ἀλκμήνη μιχθεῖσα κελαινεφέϊ Κρονίωνι·
ὃς πρὶν μὲν κατὰ γαῖαν ἀθέσφατον ἠδὲ θάλασσαν
πλαζόμενος πομπῇσιν ὑπ' Εὐρυσθῆος ἄνακτος 5
πολλὰ μὲν αὐτὸς ἔρεξεν ἀτάσθαλα, πολλὰ δ' ἀνέτλη·
νῦν δ' ἤδη κατὰ καλὸν ἕδος νιφόεντος Ὀλύμπου
ναίει τερπόμενος καὶ ἔχει καλλίσφυρον Ἥβην
Χαῖρε ἄναξ Διὸς υἱέ· δίδου δ' ἀρετήν τε καὶ ὄλβον.

XVI
To Asclepius

Ἰητῆρα νόσων Ἀσκληπιὸν ἄρχομ' ἀείδειν 1
υἱὸν Ἀπόλλωνος τὸν ἐγείνατο δῖα Κορωνὶς
Δωτίῳ ἐν πεδίῳ κούρη Φλεγύου βασιλῆος,
χάρμα μέγ' ἀνθρώποισι, κακῶν θελκτῆρ' ὀδυνάων.
Καὶ σὺ μὲν οὕτω χαῖρε ἄναξ· λίτομαι δέ σ' ἀοιδῇ. 5

XVII
To the Dioscuri

Κάστορα καὶ Πολυδεύκε' ἀείσεο Μοῦσα λίγεια, 1
Τυνδαρίδας οἳ Ζηνὸς Ὀλυμπίου ἐξεγένοντο·
τοὺς ὑπὸ Ταϋγέτου κορυφῆς τέκε πότνια Λήδη
λάθρῃ ὑποδμηθεῖσα κελαινεφέϊ Κρονίωνι.
Χαίρετε Τυνδαρίδαι, ταχέων ἐπιβήτορες ἵππων. 5

XVIII
To Hermes

Ἑρμῆν ἀείδω Κυλλήνιον Ἀργειφόντην 1
Κυλλήνης μεδέοντα καὶ Ἀρκαδίης πολυμήλου,
ἄγγελον ἀθανάτων ἐριούνιον ὃν τέκε Μαῖα
Ἄτλαντος θυγάτηρ Διὸς ἐν φιλότητι μιγεῖσα
αἰδοίη· μακάρων δὲ θεῶν ἀλέεινεν ὅμιλον 5
ἄντρῳ ναιετάουσα παλισκίῳ ἔνθα Κρονίων
νύμφῃ ἐϋπλοκάμῳ μισγέσκετο νυκτὸς ἀμολγῷ,
εὖτε κατὰ γλυκὺς ὕπνος ἔχοι λευκώλενον Ἥρην·
λάνθανε δ' ἀθανάτους τε θεοὺς θνητούς τ' ἀνθρώπους.
Καὶ σὺ μὲν οὕτω χαῖρε Διὸς καὶ Μαιάδος υἱέ· 10
σεῦ δ' ἐγὼ ἀρξάμενος μεταβήσομαι ἄλλον ἐς ὕμνον.
χαῖρ' Ἑρμῆ χαριδῶτα διάκτορε, δῶτορ ἐάων.

XIX
To Pan

Ἀμφί μοι Ἑρμείαο φίλον γόνον ἔννεπε Μοῦσα, 1
αἰγιπόδην δικέρωτα φιλόκροτον ὅς τ' ἀνὰ πίση
δενδρήεντ' ἄμυδις φοιτᾷ χοροήθεσι νύμφαις
αἵ τε κατ' αἰγίλιπος πέτρης στείβουσι κάρηνα
Πᾶν' ἀνακεκλόμεναι νόμιον θεὸν ἀγλαέθειρον 5

αὐχμήενθ', ὃς πάντα λόφον νιφόεντα λέλογχε
καὶ κορυφὰς ὀρέων καὶ πετρήεντα κέλευθα.
φοιτᾷ δ' ἔνθα καὶ ἔνθα διὰ ῥωπήϊα πυκνά,
ἄλλοτε μὲν ῥείθροισιν ἐφελκόμενος μαλακοῖσιν,
ἄλλοτε δ' αὖ πέτρῃσιν ἐν ἠλιβάτοισι διοιχνεῖ, 10
ἀκροτάτην κορυφὴν μηλοσκόπον εἰσαναβαίνων.
πολλάκι δ' ἀργινόεντα διέδραμεν οὔρεα μακρά,
πολλάκι δ' ἐν κνημοῖσι διήλασε θῆρας ἐναίρων
ὀξέα δερκόμενος· τότε δ' ἕσπερος ἔκλαγεν οἷον
ἄγρης ἐξανιών, δονάκων ὕπο μοῦσαν ἀθύρων 15
νήδυμον· οὐκ ἂν τόν γε παραδράμοι ἐν μελέεσσιν
ὄρνις ἥ τ' ἔαρος πολυανθέος ἐν πετάλοισι
θρῆνον ἐπιπροχέουσ' ἀχέει μελίγηρυν ἀοιδήν.
σὺν δέ σφιν τότε νύμφαι ὀρεστιάδες λιγύμολποι
φοιτῶσαι πυκνὰ ποσσὶν ἐπὶ κρήνῃ μελανύδρῳ 20
μέλπονται, κορυφὴν δὲ περιστένει οὔρεος ἠχώ·
δαίμων δ' ἔνθα καὶ ἔνθα χορῶν τοτὲ δ' ἐς μέσον ἕρπων
πυκνὰ ποσὶν διέπει, λαῖφος δ' ἐπὶ νῶτα δαφοινὸν
λυγκὸς ἔχει λιγυρῇσιν ἀγαλλόμενος φρένα μολπαῖς
ἐν μαλακῷ λειμῶνι τόθι κρόκος ἠδ' ὑάκινθος 25
εὐώδης θαλέθων καταμίσγεται ἄκριτα ποίῃ.
ὑμνεῦσιν δὲ θεοὺς μάκαρας καὶ μακρὸν Ὄλυμπον·
οἷόν θ' Ἑρμείην ἐριούνιον ἔξοχον ἄλλων
ἔννεπον ὡς ὅ γ' ἅπασι θεοῖς θοὸς ἄγγελός ἐστι
καί ῥ' ὅ γ' ἐς Ἀρκαδίην πολυπίδακα, μητέρα μήλων, 30
ἐξίκετ', ἔνθα τέ οἱ τέμενος Κυλληνίου ἐστίν.
ἔνθ' ὅ γε καὶ θεὸς ὢν ψαφαρότριχα μῆλ' ἐνόμευεν
ἀνδρὶ πάρα θνητῷ· θάλε γὰρ πόθος ὑγρὸς ἐπελθὼν
νύμφῃ ἐϋπλοκάμῳ Δρύοπος φιλότητι μιγῆναι·
ἐκ δ' ἐτέλεσσε γάμον θαλερόν, τέκε δ' ἐν μεγάροισιν 35
Ἑρμείῃ φίλον υἱὸν ἄφαρ τερατωπὸν ἰδέσθαι,
αἰγιπόδην δικέρωτα πολύκροτον ἡδυγέλωτα·
φεῦγε δ' ἀναΐξασα, λίπεν δ' ἄρα παῖδα τιθήνη·
δεῖσε γὰρ ὡς ἴδεν ὄψιν ἀμείλιχον ἠϋγένειον.
τὸν δ' αἶψ' Ἑρμείας ἐριούνιος εἰς χέρα θῆκε 40
δεξάμενος, χαῖρεν δὲ νόῳ περιώσια δαίμων.
ῥίμφα δ' ἐς ἀθανάτων ἕδρας κίε παῖδα καλύψας
δέρμασιν ἐν πυκινοῖσιν ὀρεσκῴοιο λαγωοῦ·
πὰρ δὲ Ζηνὶ καθῖζε καὶ ἄλλοις ἀθανάτοισιν,
δεῖξε δὲ κοῦρον ἑόν· πάντες δ' ἄρα θυμὸν ἔτερφθεν 45
ἀθάνατοι, περίαλλα δ' ὁ Βάκχειος Διόνυσος·
Πᾶνα δέ μιν καλέεσκον ὅτι φρένα πᾶσιν ἔτερψε.

Καὶ σὺ μὲν οὕτω χαῖρε ἄναξ, ἵλαμαι δέ σ' ἀοιδῇ·
αὐτὰρ ἐγὼ καὶ σεῖο καὶ ἄλλης μνήσομ' ἀοιδῆς.

XX
To Hephaestus

Ἥφαιστον κλυτόμητιν ἀείδεο Μοῦσα λίγεια, 1
ὅς μετ' Ἀθηναίης γλαυκώπιδος ἀγλαὰ ἔργα
ἀνθρώπους ἐδίδαξεν ἐπὶ χθονός, οἳ τὸ πάρος περ
ἄντροις ναιετάασκον ἐν οὔρεσιν ἠΰτε θῆρες.
νῦν δὲ δι' Ἥφαιστον κλυτοτέχνην ἔργα δαέντες 5
ῥηϊδίως αἰῶνα τελεσφόρον εἰς ἐνιαυτὸν
εὔκηλοι διάγουσιν ἐνὶ σφετέροισι δόμοισιν.
Ἀλλ' ἵληθ' Ἥφαιστε· δίδου δ' ἀρετήν τε καὶ ὄλβον.

XXI
To Apollo

Φοῖβε σὲ μὲν καὶ κύκνος ὑπὸ πτερύγων λιγ' ἀείδει 1
ὄχθῃ ἐπιθρῴσκων ποταμὸν πάρα δινήεντα
Πηνειόν· σὲ δ' ἀοιδὸς ἔχων φόρμιγγα λίγειαν
ἡδυεπὴς πρῶτόν τε καὶ ὕστατον αἰὲν ἀείδει.
Καὶ σὺ μὲν οὕτω χαῖρε ἄναξ, ἵλαμαι δέ σ' ἀοιδῇ. 5

XXII
To Poseidon

Ἀμφὶ Ποσειδάωνα θεὸν μέγαν ἄρχομ' ἀείδειν 1
γαίης κινητῆρα καὶ ἀτρυγέτοιο θαλάσσης
πόντιον, ὅς θ' Ἑλικῶνα καὶ εὐρείας ἔχει Αἰγάς.
διχθά τοι Ἐννοσίγαιε θεοὶ τιμὴν ἐδάσαντο
ἵππων τε δμητῆρ' ἔμεναι σωτῆρά τε νηῶν. 5
Χαῖρε Ποσείδαον γαιήοχε κυανοχαῖτα,
καὶ μάκαρ εὐμενὲς ἦτορ ἔχων πλώουσιν ἄρηγε.

XXIII
To Zeus

Ζῆνα θεῶν τὸν ἄριστον ἀείσομαι ἠδὲ μέγιστον 1
εὐρύοπα κρείοντα τελεσφόρον, ὅς τε Θέμιστι
ἐγκλιδὸν ἑζομένῃ πυκινοὺς ὀάρους ὀαρίζει.

Ἴληθ' εὐρύοπα Κρονίδη κύδιστε μέγιστε.

XXIV
To Hestia

Ἑστίη, ἥ τε ἄνακτος Ἀπόλλωνος ἑκάτοιο 1
Πυθοῖ ἐν ἠγαθέῃ ἱερὸν δόμον ἀμφιπολεύεις,
αἰεὶ σῶν πλοκάμων ἀπολείβεται ὑγρὸν ἔλαιον·
ἔρχεο τόνδ' ἀνὰ οἶκον, ἐπέρχεο θυμὸν ἔχουσα
σὺν Διὶ μητιόεντι· χάριν δ' ἅμ' ὄπασσον ἀοιδῇ. 5

XXV
To the Muses and Apollo

Μουσάων ἄρχωμαι Ἀπόλλωνός τε Διός τε· 1
ἐκ γὰρ Μουσάων καὶ ἑκηβόλου Ἀπόλλωνος
ἄνδρες ἀοιδοὶ ἔασιν ἐπὶ χθονὶ καὶ κιθαρισταί,
ἐκ δὲ Διὸς βασιλῆες· ὁ δ' ὄλβιος ὅν τινα Μοῦσαι
φίλωνται· γλυκερή οἱ ἀπὸ στόματος ῥέει αὐδή. 5
Χαίρετε τέκνα Διὸς καὶ ἐμὴν τιμήσατ' ἀοιδήν·
αὐτὰρ ἐγὼν ὑμέων τε καὶ ἄλλης μνήσομ' ἀοιδῆς.

XXVI
To Dionysus

Κισσοκόμην Διόνυσον ἐρίβρομον ἄρχομ' ἀείδειν 1
Ζηνὸς καὶ Σεμέλης ἐρικυδέος ἀγλαὸν υἱόν,
ὃν τρέφον ἠΰκομοι νύμφαι παρὰ πατρὸς ἄνακτος
δεξάμεναι κόλποισι καὶ ἐνδυκέως ἀτίταλλον
Νύσης ἐν γυάλοις· ὁ δ' ἀέξετο πατρὸς ἕκητι 5
ἄντρῳ ἐν εὐώδει μεταρίθμιος ἀθανάτοισιν.
αὐτὰρ ἐπεὶ δὴ τόνδε θεαὶ πολύυμνον ἔθρεψαν,
δὴ τότε φοιτίζεσκε καθ' ὑλήεντας ἐναύλους
κισσῷ καὶ δάφνῃ πεπυκασμένος· αἱ δ' ἅμ' ἕποντο
νύμφαι, ὁ δ' ἐξηγεῖτο· βρόμος δ' ἔχεν ἄσπετον ὕλην. 10
Καὶ σὺ μὲν οὕτω χαῖρε πολυστάφυλ' ὦ Διόνυσε·
δὸς δ' ἡμᾶς χαίροντας ἐς ὥρας αὖτις ἱκέσθαι,
ἐκ δ' αὖθ' ὡράων εἰς τοὺς πολλοὺς ἐνιαυτούς.

XXVII
To Artemis

Ἄρτεμιν ἀείδω χρυσηλάκατον κελαδεινὴν 1
παρθένον αἰδοίην ἐλαφηβόλον ἰοχέαιραν
αὐτοκασιγνήτην χρυσαόρου Ἀπόλλωνος,
ἣ κατ᾽ ὄρη σκιόεντα καὶ ἄκριας ἠνεμοέσσας
ἄγρῃ τερπομένη παγχρύσεα τόξα τιταίνει 5
πέμπουσα στονόεντα βέλη· τρομέει δὲ κάρηνα
ὑψηλῶν ὀρέων, ἰαχεῖ δ᾽ ἔπι δάσκιος ὕλη
δεινὸν ὑπὸ κλαγγῆς θηρῶν, φρίσσει δέ τε γαῖα
πόντος τ᾽ ἰχθυόεις· ἡ δ᾽ ἄλκιμον ἦτορ ἔχουσα
πάντῃ ἐπιστρέφεται θηρῶν ὀλέκουσα γενέθλην. 10
αὐτὰρ ἐπὴν τερφθῇ θηροσκόπος ἰοχέαιρα
εὐφρήνῃ δὲ νόον χαλάσασ᾽ εὐκαμπέα τόξα,
ἔρχεται ἐς μέγα δῶμα κασιγνήτοιο φίλοιο
Φοίβου Ἀπόλλωνος Δελφῶν ἐς πίονα δῆμον
Μουσῶν καὶ Χαρίτων καλὸν χορὸν ἀρτυνέουσα. 15
ἔνθα κατακρεμάσασα παλίντονα τόξα καὶ ἰοὺς
ἡγεῖται χαρίεντα περὶ χροῒ κόσμον ἔχουσα,
ἐξάρχουσα χορούς· αἱ δ᾽ ἀμβροσίην ὄπ᾽ ἰεῖσαι
ὑμνεῦσιν Λητὼ καλλίσφυρον ὡς τέκε παῖδας
ἀθανάτων βουλῇ τε καὶ ἔργμασιν ἔξοχ᾽ ἀρίστους, 20
Χαίρετε τέκνα Διὸς καὶ Λητοῦς ἠϋκόμοιο·
αὐτὰρ ἐγὼν ὑμέων καὶ ἄλλης μνήσομ᾽ ἀοιδῆς.

XXVIII
To Athena

Παλλάδ᾽ Ἀθηναίην κυδρὴν θεὸν ἄρχομ᾽ ἀείδειν 1
γλαυκῶπιν πολύμητιν ἀμείλιχον ἦτορ ἔχουσαν
παρθένον αἰδοίην ἐρυσίπτολιν ἀλκήεσσαν
Τριτογενῆ, τὴν αὐτὸς ἐγείνατο μητίετα Ζεὺς
σεμνῆς ἐκ κεφαλῆς, πολεμήϊα τεύχε᾽ ἔχουσαν 5
χρύσεα παμφανόωντα· σέβας δ᾽ ἔχε πάντας ὁρῶντας
ἀθανάτους· ἡ δὲ πρόσθεν Διὸς αἰγιόχοιο
ἐσσυμένως ὤρουσεν ἀπ᾽ ἀθανάτοιο καρήνου
σείσασ᾽ ὀξὺν ἄκοντα· μέγας δ᾽ ἐλελίζετ᾽ Ὄλυμπος
δεινὸν ὑπὸ βρίμης γλαυκώπιδος, ἀμφὶ δὲ γαῖα 10
σμερδαλέον ἰάχησεν, ἐκινήθη δ᾽ ἄρα πόντος
κύμασι πορφυρέοισι κυκώμενος, ἔσχετο δ᾽ ἅλμη

ἐξαπίνης· στῆσεν δ' Ὑπερίονος ἀγλαὸς υἱὸς
ἵππους ὠκύποδας δηρὸν χρόνον εἰσότε κούρη
εἵλετ' ἀπ' ἀθανάτων ὤμων θεοείκελα τεύχη 15
Παλλὰς Ἀθηναίη· γήθησε δὲ μητίετα Ζεύς.
Καὶ σὺ μὲν οὕτω χαῖρε Διὸς τέκος αἰγιόχοιο·
αὐτὰρ ἐγὼ καὶ σεῖο καὶ ἄλλης μνήσομ' ἀοιδῆς.

XXIX
To Hestia

Ἑστίη ἣ πάντων ἐν δώμασιν ὑψηλοῖσιν 1
ἀθανάτων τε θεῶν χαμαὶ ἐρχομένων τ' ἀνθρώπων
ἕδρην ἀίδιον ἔλαχες πρεσβηΐδα τιμὴν
καλὸν ἔχουσα γέρας καὶ τιμήν· οὐ γὰρ ἄτερ σοῦ
εἰλαπίναι θνητοῖσιν ἵν' οὐ πρώτῃ πυμάτῃ τε 5
Ἑστίῃ ἀρχόμενος σπένδει μελιηδέα οἶνον·
καὶ σύ μοι Ἀργειφόντα Διὸς καὶ Μαιάδος υἱὲ
ἄγγελε τῶν μακάρων χρυσόρραπι δῶτορ ἐάων,
ναίετε δώματα καλά, φίλα φρεσὶν ἀλλήλοισιν

ἵλαος ὢν ἐπάρηγε σὺν αἰδοίῃ τε φίλῃ τε 10
Ἑστίῃ· ἀμφότεροι γὰρ ἐπιχθονίων ἀνθρώπων
εἰδότες ἔργματα καλὰ νόῳ θ' ἕσπεσθε καὶ ἥβῃ.
Χαῖρε Κρόνου θύγατερ, σύ τε καὶ χρυσόρραπις Ἑρμῆς.
αὐτὰρ ἐγὼν ὑμέων τε καὶ ἄλλης μνήσομ' ἀοιδῆς.

XXX
To Earth, Mother of All

Γαῖαν παμμήτειραν ἀείσομαι ἠϋθέμεθλον 1
πρεσβίστην, ἣ φέρβει ἐπὶ χθονὶ πάνθ' ὁπόσ' ἐστίν·
ἠμὲν ὅσα χθόνα δῖαν ἐπέρχεται ἠδ' ὅσα πόντον
ἠδ' ὅσα πωτῶνται, τάδε φέρβεται ἐκ σέθεν ὄλβου.
ἐκ σέο δ' εὔπαιδές τε καὶ εὔκαρποι τελέθουσι 5
πότνια, σεῦ δ' ἔχεται δοῦναι βίον ἠδ' ἀφελέσθαι
θνητοῖς ἀνθρώποισιν· ὁ δ' ὄλβιος ὅν κε σὺ θυμῷ
πρόφρων τιμήσῃς· τῷ τ' ἄφθονα πάντα πάρεστι.
βρίθει μέν σφιν ἄρουρα φερέσβιος, ἠδὲ κατ' ἀγροὺς
κτήνεσιν εὐθηνεῖ, οἶκος δ' ἐμπίπλαται ἐσθλῶν· 10
αὐτοὶ δ' εὐνομίῃσι πόλιν κάτα καλλιγύναικα
κοιρανέουσ'· ὄλβος δὲ πολὺς καὶ πλοῦτος ὀπηδεῖ·
παῖδες δ' εὐφροσύνῃ νεοθηλέϊ κυδιόωσι,

παρθενικαί τε χοροῖς φερεσανθέσιν εὔφρονι θυμῷ
παίζουσαι σκαίρουσι κατ' ἄνθεα μαλθακὰ ποίης, 15
οὕς κε σὺ τιμήσῃς σεμνὴ θεὰ ἄφθονε δαῖμον.
Χαῖρε θεῶν μήτηρ, ἄλοχ' Οὐρανοῦ ἀστερόεντος,
πρόφρων δ' ἀντ' ᾠδῆς βίοτον θυμήρε' ὄπαζε·
αὐτὰρ ἐγὼ καὶ σεῖο καὶ ἄλλης μνήσομ' ἀοιδῆς.

XXXI
To Helios

Ἥλιον ὑμνεῖν αὖτε Διὸς τέκος ἄρχεο Μοῦσα 1
Καλλιόπη φαέθοντα, τὸν Εὐρυφάεσσα βοῶπις
γείνατο Γαίης παιδὶ καὶ Οὐρανοῦ ἀστερόεντος·
γῆμε γὰρ Εὐρυφάεσσαν ἀγακλειτὴν Ὑπερίων
αὐτοκασιγνήτην, ἥ οἱ τέκε κάλλιμα τέκνα 5
Ἠῶ τε ῥοδόπηχυν ἐϋπλόκαμόν τε Σελήνην
Ἠέλιόν τ' ἀκάμαντ' ἐπιείκελον ἀθανάτοισιν,
ὃς φαίνει θνητοῖσι καὶ ἀθανάτοισι θεοῖσιν
ἵπποις ἐμβεβαώς· σμερδνὸν δ' ὅ γε δέρκεται ὄσσοις
χρυσῆς ἐκ κόρυθος, λαμπραὶ δ' ἀκτῖνες ἀπ' αὐτοῦ 10
αἰγλῆεν στίλβουσι, παρὰ κροτάφων τε παρειαὶ
λαμπραὶ ἀπὸ κρατὸς χαρίεν κατέχουσι πρόσωπον
τηλαυγές· καλὸν δὲ περὶ χροῒ λάμπεται ἔσθος
λεπτουργὲς πνοιῇ ἀνέμων, ὑπὸ δ' ἄρσενες ἵπποι

ἔνθ' ἄρ' ὅ γε στήσας χρυσόζυγον ἅρμα καὶ ἵππους 15
θεσπέσιος πέμπῃσι δι' οὐρανοῦ ὠκεανὸν δέ.
Χαῖρε ἄναξ, πρόφρων δὲ βίον θυμήρε' ὄπαζε·
ἐκ σέο δ' ἀρξάμενος κλῄσω μερόπων γένος ἀνδρῶν
ἡμιθέων ὧν ἔργα θεοὶ θνητοῖσιν ἔδειξαν.

XXXII
To Selene

Μήνην ἀείδειν τανυσίπτερον ἔσπετε Μοῦσαι 1
ἡδυεπεῖς κοῦραι Κρονίδεω Διὸς ἴστορες ᾠδῆς·
ἧς ἄπο αἴγλη γαῖαν ἑλίσσεται οὐρανόδεικτος
κρατὸς ἀπ' ἀθανάτοιο, πολὺς δ' ὑπὸ κόσμος ὄρωρεν
αἴγλης λαμπούσης· στίλβει δέ τ' ἀλάμπετος ἀὴρ 5
χρυσέου ἀπὸ στεφάνου, ἀκτῖνες δ' ἐνδιάονται,
εὖτ' ἂν ἀπ' Ὠκεανοῖο λοεσσαμένη χρόα καλὸν
εἵματα ἑσσαμένη τηλαυγέα δῖα Σελήνη

ζευξαμένη πώλους ἐριαύχενας αἰγλήεντας
ἐσσυμένως προτέρωσ' ἐλάσῃ καλλίτριχας ἵππους 10
ἑσπερίη διχόμηνος· ὅ τε πλήθει μέγας ὄγμος,
λαμπρόταταί τ' αὐγαὶ τότ' ἀεξομένης τελέθουσιν
οὐρανόθεν· τέκμωρ δὲ βροτοῖς καὶ σῆμα τέτυκται.
τῇ ῥά ποτε Κρονίδης ἐμίγη φιλότητι καὶ εὐνῇ·
ἡ δ' ὑποκυσαμένη Πανδείην γείνατο κούρην 15
ἐκπρεπὲς εἶδος ἔχουσαν ἐν ἀθανάτοισι θεοῖσι.
Χαῖρε ἄνασσα θεὰ λευκώλενε δῖα Σελήνη
πρόφρον ἐϋπλόκαμος· σέο δ' ἀρχόμενος κλέα φωτῶν
ᾄσομαι ἡμιθέων ὧν κλείουσ' ἔργματ' ἀοιδοὶ
Μουσάων θεράποντες ἀπὸ στομάτων ἐροέντων.

XXXIII
To the Dioscuri

Ἀμφὶ Διὸς κούρους ἑλικώπιδες ἔσπετε Μοῦσαι 1
Τυνδαρίδας Λήδης καλλισφύρου ἀγλαὰ τέκνα,
Κάστορά θ' ἱππόδαμον καὶ ἀμώμητον Πολυδεύκεα,
τοὺς ὑπὸ Ταϋγέτου κορυφῇ ὄρεος μεγάλοιο
μιχθεῖσ' ἐν φιλότητι κελαινεφέϊ Κρονίωνι 5
σωτῆρας τέκε παῖδας ἐπιχθονίων ἀνθρώπων
ὠκυπόρων τε νεῶν, ὅτε τε σπέρχωσιν ἄελλαι
χειμέριαι κατὰ πόντον ἀμείλιχον· οἱ δ' ἀπὸ νηῶν
εὐχόμενοι καλέουσι Διὸς κούρους μεγάλοιο
ἄρνεσσιν λευκοῖσιν ἐπ' ἀκρωτήρια βάντες 10
πρύμνης· τὴν δ' ἄνεμός τε μέγας καὶ κῦμα θαλάσσης
θῆκαν ὑποβρυχίην, οἱ δ' ἐξαπίνης ἐφάνησαν
ξουθῇσι πτερύγεσσι δι' αἰθέρος ἀΐξαντες,
αὐτίκα δ' ἀργαλέων ἀνέμων κατέπαυσαν ἀέλλας,
κύματα δ' ἐστόρεσαν λευκῆς ἁλὸς ἐν πελάγεσσι, 15
ναύταις σήματα καλὰ πόνου σφίσιν· οἱ δὲ ἰδόντες
γήθησαν, παύσαντο δ' ὀϊζυροῖο πόνοιο.
Χαίρετε Τυνδαρίδαι ταχέων ἐπιβήτορες ἵππων·
αὐτὰρ ἐγὼν ὑμέων καὶ ἄλλης μνήσομ' ἀοιδῆς.

XXXIV
To My Hosts

Αἰδεῖσθε ξενίων κεχρημένον ἠδὲ δόμοιο 1
οἳ πόλιν αἰπεινὴν νύμφης ἐρατώπιδος Ἥρης
ναίετε, Σαιδήνης πόδα νείατον ὑψικόμοιο,

ἀμβρόσιον πίνοντες ὕδωρ ξανθοῦ ποταμοῖο
Ἕρμου καλὰ ῥέοντος ὃν ἀθάνατος τέκετο Ζεύς. 5
———

COMMENTARY

The text used is that of T. W. Allen (Oxford 1946).

Abbreviations:

AHS   T. W. Allen, W. R. Halliday and E. E. Sikes, The Homeric Hymns (Oxford 1936)

GP   J. D. Denniston, Greek Particles (Oxford 1954)

S   H. W. Smyth, Greek Grammar, revised by G. Messing (Cambridge, Mass. 1956)

<   "(is) from"

Roman numerals without further specification (e.g. VI.20) refer to individual Homeric Hymns.

Students who have some knowledge of Italian may find F. Cassola, Inni Omerici (Verona, 1975) useful.

I

Two fragments of a hymn to Dionysus. The first nine lines are quoted by the historian Diodorus Siculus (first century B.C.). The rest appear in the Moscow manuscript of the Hymns.

1-9 A list of places where men say Dionysus was born. Dracanon is a promontory on the island of Cos at the southwestern corner of Turkey; Icaros is an island near Samos; Naxos is the island at the center of the Cyclades where Dionysus was said to have found the princess Ariadne after she had been deserted by Theseus (Odyssey XI.320ff.); the Alpheus River is in Elis near Olympia in the western Peloponnese; Thebes is the city in Boeotia where Euripides' Bacchae takes place; of several places named Nysa, the poet of this hymn chooses the one in Libya.

2. εἰραφιῶτα: vocative < εἰραφιώτης, "sewn in"; an epithet of Dionysus. The mortal Semele asked her lover Zeus to make love to her as he did to his wife Hera. The lightning flash killed her, but Zeus snatched the embryonic Dionysus from her womb, sewed him into his thigh, and carried him to term there.

3. βαθυδινήεντι: "deep-eddying."

4. κυσαμένην< κύω, "bear in the womb." The aorist middle is used ingressively to mean "conceive."
   τερπικεραύνῳ: "delighting in thunder," a common epithet of Zeus.

5. ἄναξ: vocative.

7. πολλὸν ἀπ(ὸ) ἀνθρώπων: "far from men"; πολλόν is adverbial acc. (S 1606-11).
   κρύπτων λευκώλενον Ἥρην: "concealing (it) from white-armed Hera"; κρύπτω governs a double accusative.

9. **Φοινίκης**: Phoenicia, the coastal region centered around modern Lebanon.
   Αἰγύπτοιο ῥοάων: "the streams of Egypt," i.e., the many mouths of the Nile.

10. **οἱ**: "to her," i.e., Semele.

11. **τάμεν**: unaugmented aor. < τέμνω, "cut."
    πάντως: with σοί, "to you especially."
    τριετηρίσιν: "at biennial festivals." In counting from one event to the next, the Greeks counted both the beginning and end of the series, so that an event that we would describe as occurring every other year was to them a triennial event.

12. **τεληέσσας ἑκατόμβας**: "perfect hecatombs." "Hecatomb," literally an offering of a hundred oxen, was used of any large public sacrifice.

13. **Κρονίων**: "the son of Kronos," i.e., Zeus. A nod of the supreme god's head was enough to establish a divine ordinance.

15. **κρατός**< κράς, "head."
    ἐλέλιξεν: "set whirling," < ἐλελίζω.

16. **καρήατι**: "with his head," < κάρη.
    μητίετα= epic for μητιέτης, "devising, wise," a regular epithet for Zeus.

17. **ἵληθ(ι)**: "be favorable"; imperative < ἵλημι.
    γυναιμανές: "woman-maddener"; vocative. The release offered by the frenzied rites of Dionysus had particular appeal to women.

18. **οὐδέ πῃ ἔστι**: "nor is it in any way possible."

19. **σεῖ(ο)**< σύ; genitive after ἐπιληθομένῳ (< ἐπιλανθάνομαι, "forget"), S 1356.

21. **ἥν περ**: "the very one whom."
    Θυώνην: "Thyone," another name for Semele.

VI

A hymn to Aphrodite, goddess of love and sexuality. Lines 19-20 show that this hymn was composed for a contest. The dressing of Aphrodite by the Hours and Graces is mentioned in the long Hymn to Aphrodite (V.61-62), and Athenaeus 15.30 (second century A.D.) says that it was treated at some length in the Cypria, a poem of the so-called Epic Cycle.

1. χρυσοστέφανον: "gold-crowned." Compound adjectives often have no separate feminine endings (S 288).

2. ᾄσομαι = ἀείσομαι, < ἀείδω.
 κρήδεμνα: "battlements," i.e., towns, a doubly metaphorical extension of the basic meaning of κρήδεμνον, "headdress."
 λέλογχεν: perfect of λαγχάνω; "has as her portion."

3. εἰναλίης < ἐνάλιος, "in the sea."
 ὅθι: "where."
 μιν: an Ionic accusative singular used for all genders of the 3rd pers. sg. pronoun.
 Ζεφύρου μένος = Ζέφυρος.
 ὑγρόν: agrees with μένος.
 ἀέντος: present active participle of ἄημι, "blow."

4. ἤνεικεν< φέρω.
 κατὰ κῦμα: "over the waves."
 πολυφλοίσβοιο: "loud-roaring"; for the declension, see "The Language of the Hymns," III.1.

5. ἀφρῷ ἔνι: i.e., ἐν τῷ ἀφρῷ; for the etymology of Ἀφροδίτη "born from foam" (ἀφρός), see Hesiod, Theogony 190ff.
 τὴν= αὐτήν; see "The Language of the Hymns" IV.2 and S 1099ff.
 χρυσάμπυκες: The ἄμπυξ was a band which held back women's hair in front.

6. δέξαντ(ο): aor. without the augment, as frequently in epic.
 περί: an adverb with ἕσσαν, 1st aor. of ἕννυμι, "clothe." See "The Language of the Hymns," V.2 and S 1638.

7. κρατὶ δ' ἐπ': i.e., ἐπὶ δὲ κρατί; in poetry, prepositions are frequently placed between noun and adjective.

The Shorter Homeric Hymns

8. τρητοῖσι λοβοῖσιν: "pierced ear lobes"; for the ending, see "The Language of the Hymns," III.2.

9. ἄνθεμ(α): i.e., ἄνθεα. Several examples of elaborate earrings survive from the Archaic Period as well as from the Bronze Age, and cult statues frequently have holes where jewelry was attached.
ὀρειχάλκου: "orichalcum," an unknown metal.

11. ὅρμοισι< ὅρμος, "chain" or "necklace."
ἐκόσμεον: Supply αὐτήν; note the shift to imperfect in a description (S 1898).
οἷσι περ: "just the ones with which"; the "determinative περ" (GP 482).

12. κοσμείσθην: imperfect passive 3rd pers. dual in an indefinite temporal sentence (S 2414). In Greek art the Seasons are often portrayed as a pair.
ὁππότ(ε) ἴοιεν: "when they go"; ἴοιεν (< εἶμι, optative in a past indefinite temporal clause, S 2394) is pl. despite κοσμείσθην, but a shift from dual to pl. is common, and in later epic the dual has lost its force and can be used for a pl.

13. πατρός: Zeus. According to Hesiod, Theogony 901, the Horae were the children of Zeus and Themis.

14. χροί< χρώς, "skin."
κόσμον: predicate accusative; "when they had set everything in order."

15. οἱ δ(έ): the gods. The pronoun with δέ regularly indicates a change of subject.

16. ἐδεξιόωντο: uncontracted 3rd pers. pl. imperfect < δεξιόομαι, "to greet with the right hand."
ἕκαστος: sg. but used quite naturally as subject of ἠρήσαντο, aorist middle < ἀράομαι, "beg." Supply "her" as object.

18. Κυθερείης: "Cythereia," from Cythera, an island off Cape Malea, the southernmost point of mainland Greece, where, according to Hesiod, Theogony 192, Aphrodite was born.

19. ἑλικοβλέφαρε< ἕλιξ, "spiral," + βλέφαρον, "eyelid," meaning something like "almond-eyed," or perhaps "with fluttering lids" (cf. ἑλίσσω, "move rapidly").

γλυκυμείλιχε: "sweet and gentle."
φέρεσθαι: the epexegetical or explaining infinitive (S 2001, 2004) with δὸς (μοι) νίκην; "give (me) victory to carry away."

20. ἔντυνον: aor. imperative < ἐντύνω; it does not mean "make" or "inspire," as AHS suggest, but "make ready," "prepare." The poet asks for divine aid for the song he is about to give (ἄλλης . . . ἀοιδῆς 21), for which the present hymn is a προοίμιον.

21. A formula of closing which recurs at the end of II, X, XIX, XXVIII, and XXX, and with pl. ὑμέων for sg. σεῖο at XXV, XXVII, XXIX, and XXXIII. σεῖο and ἀοιδῆς are genitives with a verb of remembering; cf. on I.19.

VII

The story of Dionysus and the pirates is mentioned by Euripides, <u>Cyclops</u> 11-16, Ovid, <u>Metamorphoses</u> III.582-691, and others.

1. Cf. the beginnings of XIX, XXII, and XXXIII.
Σεμέλης ἐρικυδέος: "glorious Semele." See on I.2.
ὡς ἐφάνη: parallel to υἱόν; "I shall recall him, how he appeared . . ."; ἐφάνη is aorist pass. < φαίνω.
θῖν(α)< θίς, "beach, shore."

2. ἀτρυγέτοιο: "barren"(?); a Homeric adjective applied to sea and sky.

3. ἀκτῇ: governed by ἐπί.
προβλῆτι: "jutting."
νεηνίῃ = νεανίᾳ, "young man," used here as an adjective = νέῳ, "young." The phrase depends on ἐοικώς, "like, resembling."

4. πρωθήβῃ: "in first youth."
περισσείοντο: metrically convenient lengthening for περισείοντο < περισείω, "shake about"; cf. ἐϋσσέλμου = εὐσέλμου below (6).

5. περί: probably the preposition rather than adverbial with ἔχειν.

ἐϋσσέλμου = ἐϋσσέλμου, "well-benched"; the diaeresis over the upsilon indicates that the word is to be read with four syllables ("Language of the Hymns" I.2).

7. ληϊσταί: "pirates"; trisyllabic. Note the emphatic position of ληϊσταί and Τυρσηνοί at the beginnings of successive lines.

8. Τυρσηνοί: usually "Etruscans" but here it may refer to the non-Hellenic inhabitants of Thrace, Lemnos, and Athens (see AHS).
τοὺς . . . οἱ: pronouns.
μόρος = μοῖρα.

9. ἔκθορον: unaugmented aorist < ἐκθρώσκω, "jump out" (of the ship); see "Language of the Hymns" V.1.

10. εἷσαν: aorist < ἵζω, "put, lay"; supply αὐτόν, i.e., Διόνυσον, with both ἑλόντες and εἷσαν.
κεχαρημένοι: "rejoicing at heart"; < χαίρω. ἦτορ is the acc. of respect, commonly used with parts of the body (S 1601a).

11. μιν: here = αὐτόν; see "Language of the Hymns" IV.1.

13. λύγοι: "withies," thin wands of willow.
ἀπό: adverbial with ἔπιπτον; "Language of the Hymns" V.2.

14. χειρῶν and ποδῶν: genitives of separation with ἀπὸ τηλόσ' ἔπιπτον.
ἠδέ: "and."

15. ὄμμασι: with μειδιάων.

16. οἷς: "his" (companions); in epic, ὅς, ἥ, ὅν is used as a possessive pronoun (S 330d).
ἐκέκλετο: epic aorist < κέλομαι, "urge, exhort"; used with dative.

17. Δαιμόνιοι: "good sirs."
τίνα τόνδε: "whom this?" i.e. "who is this whom?"
δεσμεύεθ' = δεσμεύετε, with elision of the final vowel and aspiration of the τ before the rough breathing of ἑλόντες (S 124).

20. ἠέ = ἤ.

22. ἀλλ(ὰ) ἄγετ(ε): "come on now"; ἄγε/ἄγετε frequently supplement imperatives or hortatory subjunctives (here, ἀφῶμεν < ἀφίημι).

23. μηδ' ἐπὶ χεῖρας ἰάλλετε: "and don't lay a hand on him;" ἐπί is adverbial.
τι: adverbial, "in some way."

24. λαίλαπα < λαῖλαψ, "tempest."

25. ἀρχός: the captain.
ἠνίπαπε < ἐνίπτω, "rebuke."

26. οὖρον: "fair wind."

26f. ἱστίον . . . λαβών: "take all the rigging (ὅπλα) and hoist (ἕλκεο = ἕλκεσο, 2nd pers. sg. imperative < ἕλκω) the sail."
αὖτ(ε)· "on the other hand."

28. Αἴγυπτον: acc. of place often has no preposition in poetry (S 1588).

29. Ὑπερβορέους: A mythical race "beyond the North Wind (Βορέας)."
ἢ ἑκαστέρω: "or farther"; comparative < ἑκάς.
ἐς . . . τελευτήν: "finally."

30. ἐκ: adverbial.
ἐρεῖ: "he will tell"; future of a rare present εἴρω.

31. οὕς: possessive. See on 16.

33. ἀμφί: adverb.

34. καττάνυσαν: unaugmented aorist < κατατανύω, "stretch tight."

36. κελάρυζ(ε): unaugmented imperfect < κελαρύζω, "babble," "murmur."

37. τάφος: "astonishment."

38. ἀκρότατον ... ἱστίον: "top of the sail."

39f. ἄμπελος, βότρυες, κισσός: The vine, grape-cluster, and ivy are all associated with Dionysus.

39. κατεκρημνῶντο: "were hanging down"; imperfect < κατακρημνάομαι = κατακρήμναμαι.

41. ἐπί: adverbial with ὀρώρει, "sprang up," pluperfect < ὄρνυμι.

42. σκαλμοί: "oarlocks."

43. νῆ(α): object of ἰδόντες.
ἤδη τότ' ἔπειτα: "then, at that very moment."

44. πελάαν: infinitive < πελάω, poetic form of πελάζω, "cause to approach."
ὁ δ': Dionysus. See on VI.15.
σφι: "before their eyes"; dative of interest (S 1474).

44f. νηὸς ... ἐπ(ὶ) ἀκροτάτης: "at the end of the ship."

45. μέγα: adverbial acc. (S 1609) with ἔβραχεν; "he roared a great roar."
ἐν μέσσῃ: "midships."

46. λασιαύχενα: "shaggy-necked."
σήματα: "signs," "portents."

47. ἄν = ἀνά, adverbial with ἔστη; the verb must be taken with both ἄρκτος and λέων--"awkwardly," as AHS say.
μεμαυῖα: "furiously eager," participle < μέμονα, a perfect with present sense.

48. δεινόν: internal acc. with ἰδών.
ὑπόδρα ἰδών: "looking sternly."
ἐφόβηθεν: 3rd pl. aorist pass. < φοβέω; with the motion implied by εἰς, translate "they went fearfully."

50. ἐκπλαγέντες: "panic-stricken," < ἐκπλήσσω.
ὁ δ': the lion.
ἐξαλύοντες: "fleeing from."

52. πήδησαν: unaugmented aorist < πηδάω, "jump down."

54. ἔσχεθε < σχέθω, "hold," "check."
    ἔθηκε: "made," as often.

55. †δῖ' ἑκάτωρ: The dagger or obelus indicates a passage that has become hopelessly corrupted as the text was copied from manuscript to manuscript. The most likely solution is to understand the vocative of δῖος followed by a proper name.

56. τέκε: unaugmented aorist < τίκτω.

57. Καδμηΐς: "daughter of Kadmos."
    μιγεῖσα: aorist pass. participle < μίγνυμι, "mingle," a euphemism for sexual intercourse.

58. οὐδέ πῃ ἔστι: See on I.18.

59. ληθόμενον< λήθω = λανθάνω.
    κοσμῆσαι: "to put in order," the right word for formulaic composition. For the closing formula compare I.18-19.

VIII

The accumulation of epithets in 1-8 and the fact that Ares is invoked as planet, not god, set this hymn apart from the rest of the collection. It has been thought to resemble the "Orphic" hymns of late antiquity, but in style and subject matter its closest counterparts are the hymns of the Neoplatonic philosopher Proclus (fifth century A.D.). See M. L. West, "The Eighth Homeric Hymn and Proclus," Classical Quarterly 20(1970), 300-304.

1-3. "Ares, exceeding strong, master of the chariot, gold-helmeted, strong-willed, shield-bearer, city-saver, bronze-armored, strong-handed, unwearied, mighty with the spear, bulwark of Olympus."

4. Νίκης: Elsewhere her father is Pallas. "The relation of Ares here to Nike and Themis is not mythological but symbolical" (AHS).
   συναρωγέ: "helper."

5. ἀντιβίοισι: "those who oppose."

6-8. πυραυγέα ... ἔχουσι: "whirling your fire-red globe among the upper air's seven-fold tracks, where your blazing steeds keep you always over the third orbit." Earth is at the center of the poet's cosmos, and the planets, including the sun and moon, circle the earth on a series of spheres or heavens. Aristotle (On the Cosmos 2, 392A) gives the order of spheres, going out from the earth, as Moon, Sun, Venus, Mercury, Mars, Jupiter, Saturn. The τριτάτη ἄντυξ is thus the third orbit from the outside.
κλῦθι: 2nd sing. aorist act. imperative of κλύω.

10. πρηΰ: "gently," adverbial acc. < πρηΰς = πρᾶος.

11. κάρτος ἀρήϊον: "strength in war"; like σέλας, object of καταστίλβων, "beaming down."

12. σεύσασθαι: "to drive off."
κακότητα: In Orphic and Neoplatonic thought κακότης is often used for the essential wickedness of existence on the earth.
ἀπατηλὸν ... ὁρμήν: "deceitful impulse."

13. ὑπογνάμψαι φρεσίν: "to bend with my mind."

14. κατισχέμεν: infinitive of κατίσχω, "check," like ἐπιβαινέμεν (15).
ἐρέθῃσι: "provokes," < ἐρέθω.

15. φυλόπιδος κρυερῆς: "(in the ways) of the blood-curdling battle-cry"; gen. with the infinitive ἐπιβαινέμεν.

16. μένειν: epexegetical infinitive elaborating on μάκαρ θάρσος, "blessed courage."

17. προφυγόντα: agrees with με understood as subject of μένειν.
μόθον: with δυσμενέων, "the battle-din of my enemies."

IX

The place-names in this hymn suggest that it was composed for a festival at Claros in Ionia, on the coast of Turkey about 30 miles south of Izmir, where there was a temple and oracle of Apollo (cf. III.40). The hymn may be intended to explain some rite in which the goddess's image was carried from the Meles to Claros, but there is no evidence except this hymn for such a rite.

1. ὕμνει: imperative.
   Ἑκάτοιο: "Far-shooter," a traditional epithet of Apollo.

2. ἰοχέαιραν: "showering arrows."
   ὁμότροφον Ἀπόλλωνος: "brought up with Apollo"; the gen. shows connection (S 1417).

3. θ'= τε and not to be translated (S 2970); it serves only to connect the relative clause ἥ . . . διώκει with the phrases in line 2.
   ἵππους: Her chariot is usually drawn by stags or deer.
   Μέλητος: gen. after ἄρσασα < ἄρδω, "water in," "water with." The identity of the Meles is much disputed; the name has been assigned to three streams flowing into the Gulf of Izmir.

4. διώκει: here "drives."

6. ἧσται: "sits"; < ἧμαι.

8. σε: with ἀείδειν.

9. σευ: gen. with ἀρξάμενος.

X

1. Κυθέραιαν: See on VI.18.
   τε: the generalizing or epic τε which does not mean "and" but simply shows that the relative clause describes a constant or general characteristic (GP 520).

2-3. ἐφ . . . μειδιάει < ἐπιμειδιάω, "smile at"; supply αὐτούς.

3. ἄνθος: "bloom"; subject of ἐπιθέει, "runs over (her face)."

4. Σαλαμῖνος: the city on Cyprus, not the island off the coast of Attica; gen. with μεδέουσα, "ruling."

ἐϋκτιμένης: "good to live in," "well-developed"; used of cities and inhabited islands and indeed of anything improved by man.

XI

Normally when the formula of transition (e.g. σεῦ δ' ἐγὼ ἀρξάμενος μεταβήσομαι ἄλλον ἐς ὕμνον) or mention of song (e.g. λίτομαι δέ σ' ἀοιδῇ) is absent, as here, it is replaced by an explicit or implied request for the divinity's help. Perhaps XI is an invocation of the goddess's protection at an assembly before battle.

1. ἐρυσίπτολιν = ἐρυσίπολιν, "city-protector."

2. πολεμήϊα: Ionic for πολέμια and pentasyllabic, as the diaeresis shows.

3. περθόμεναί τε πόληες: "cities being sacked," i.e., "the sack of cities" (S 2053).
   ἀϋτή: "war-cry."

4. ἐρρύσατο < ῥύομαι, "save," "protect."
   λαόν: properly "the people" as a war-host, like the comitia centuriata of the old Roman Republic.

5. ἄμμι = ἡμῖν; not pl. for sg., since the poet prays on behalf of the people.

XII

This hymn lacks not only the formula of transition, but also the closing address to the divinity. It may be part of a longer hymn.

2. ὑπείροχον = ὑπέροχον, "lofty," "eminent."

3. Ζηνός: gen. of Ζεύς.

4. πάντες μάκαρες: Supply θεοί.

XIII

Line 1 = II.1; line 2 = II.493; line 3 up to πόλιν = line 134 of the <u>Hymn to Demeter</u> by the Alexandrian poet Callimachus (third century B.C.).

3. σάου: 2nd sg. imperative of σαόω (= σώζω).

XIV

The Great Mother is an ancient goddess whose cult was practiced in public and private worship throughout the Mediterranean world. She appears in many forms, but the Greeks customarily identified her with Rhea, the Asiatic goddess Cybele, or Demeter.

2. λίγεια: "clear-voiced."

3. A bill of instrumentation for an orgiastic cult. κρόταλα are castanets, τύμπανα or τύπανα are small kettle-drums like the medieval European and modern Middle Eastern nakers, and αὐλοί are shawms, loud double-reed instruments usually played in pairs by a single player.

3. σύν: adverbial, "and also."

4. εὖαδεν: epic aorist < ἀνδάνω, "please"; + dat.
ἠδέ: "and"; cf. VII.14.
λεόντων: The Great Mother was mistress of wild beasts and wild places, and the lion was one of her symbols in Greek art.

XV

The epithet λεοντόθυμον, "lion-hearted," does not occur elsewhere except in Byzantine literature, but there is no other reason to think that this hymn was composed later than others in the collection.

1. μέγ(α): adverbial with ἄριστον, "best by far."
Θήβης: dat.

3. μιχθεῖσα < μίγνυμι; see on VII.57.
κελαινεφέϊ Κρονίωνι: "the cloud-black son of Cronus"; Zeus became the father of Heracles by taking on the appearance of Alcmena's husband, Amphitryon, and making love to her while Amphitryon was away on campaign.

4. πρίν: adverbial, "before."

5. πλαζόμενος: "wandering."
πομπῇσιν ὕπ(ο): "at the bidding," < πομπή, "sending forth" (cf. πέμπω).
Εὐρυσθῆος: gen.; after he had killed his wife and children in a fit of madness sent by Hera, Heracles was made to perform the famous twelve labors for King Eurystheus of Argos.

6. ἀνέτλη: "endured"; aorist as though < ἀνάτλημι (S 687).

7. νῦν δ' ἤδη: "and now"; redundant epic combination of particles.

8. Ἥβεν: After his life on earth, Heracles was deified and given Hebe (Youth personified) for his wife on Olympus.

XVI

Asclepius, son of Apollo and Coronis, daughter of the Lapith king Phlegyas, was a hero who, like Heracles, became a god. Medicine was his province, and his great temples like that at Epidaurus were centers of healing.

1. Ἰητῆρα < ἰητήρ, epic form of ἰατρός, "physician."

2. τόν: the demonstrative ὁ ἡ τό used as a relative.

3. Δωτίῳ ἐν πεδίῳ: The Dotian Plain is in Thessaly, surrounded by mountains including Ossa, Pelion, and Olympus. Some said that Asclepius was born in Thessaly, and Tricca in that region was one of his cult centers.

XVII

A hymn to Castor and Polydeuces, the Dioscuri (= Διὸς κοῦροι), sons of Zeus and Leda. This hymn is an abridgement of XXXIII. With lines 3 and 4 cf. XXXIII.4 and 5; line 5 = XXXIII.18.

1. ἀείσεο: aorist imperative middle.

2. Τυνδαρίδας: "sons of Tyndareus," the mortal husband of Leda.
   Ζηνός: "from Zeus"; gen. of the source.

3. τούς: See on XVI.2.
   Ταϋγέτου: Taygetus, a mountain west of Sparta.

4. ὑποδμηθεῖσα: aorist pass. participle < ὑποδαμάω, "overpower."

5. ἐπιβήτορες: "riders."

XVIII

A shortened version of IV; with 2-9 cf. IV.2-9, and with 10, IV.579. Line 12 looks very much like an alternate closing to be used instead of 10-11; it contains the implied request (δῶτορ ἐάων) which can replace the transitional formula in these hymns.

1 Κυλλήνιον: "the Cyllenian"; i.e. from Cyllene, a mountain in Arcadia where Hermes was said to have been born.
'Αργειφόντην: perhaps "slayer of Argus"; a traditional epithet of Hermes.

3. ἐριούνιον: another traditional epithet whose meaning is unknown. "Speedy" and "thieving" are both possible.

4. Ἄτλαντος: "of Atlas," the Titan whose daughter, the Nymph Maia, was Hermes' mother.

5. ἀλέεινεν: unaugmented imperfect < ἀλεείνω, "avoid."

6. παλισκίῳ = παλινσκίῳ, "shaded over again," "thick-shaded."

7. νυκτὸς ἀμολγῷ: perhaps "at milking-time of night," i.e., early morning or late evening.

8. κατὰ ... ἔχοι < κατέχω by tmesis.

12. χαριδῶτα: "joy-giver."
διάκτορε: "messenger."

XIX

A hymn to Pan, god of flocks (e.g. 30-33), wild places (6-14), and panic fear (38-39). Herodotus, writing in the mid-fifth century B.C., said that Pan, along with Heracles and Dionysus, was the newest of Greek gods (Hdt. II.145), and this hymn, revealing as it does a clearly developed idea of the god's origin and attributes, is not likely to have been composed earlier than the late fifth century.

1. γόνον: "offspring."

2. αἰγιπόδην δικέρωτα φιλόκροτον: "goat-footed, two-horned, lover of revels."
ὅς τ': the generalizing τε, like that in 4.
πίση = πίσεα, < πῖσος, "meadow."

3. ἄμυδις: "together with," + dat.
χοροήθεσι: "accustomed to the choral dance"; the word is found only here.

4. κατ(ά): by tmesis with στείβουσι = "tread down."
αἰγίλιπος < αἰγίλιψ, "steep," "sheer."

5. ἀνακεκλόμεναι < ἀνακέλομαι, "call on," "invoke."
ἀγλαέθειρον: "bright-haired."

6. αὐχμήενθ' = αὐχμήεντα, "squalid," with elision before a rough breathing.
λέλογχε: Ionic perfect < λαγχάνω.

8. ῥωπήϊα: "underbrush."

9. ἐφελκόμενος: "drawn to," "allured by."

11. μηλοσκόπον: "flock-lookout," really an adjective, "whence flocks are seen."

12. ἀργινόεντα: "gleaming," describing the bare upper ridges of Greek mountains as they catch the sunlight.
διέδραμεν: aorist < διατρέχω, "run across."

13. κνημοῖσι: "the lower ridges," where game is more plentiful than on the heights; < κνημός, "leg." In Greek, mountains have legs as well as foothills.
διήλασε < διελαύνω, "march through," here intransitive.
ἐναίρων: "slaying."

14. ὀξέα: adverbial acc. with δερκόμενος, "looking sharply."
τότε δ': "but then."
ἕσπερος . . . οἷον (= μόνον): "only at evening" (AHS).
ἔκλαγεν: "whistled," 2nd aorist < κλάζω.

15. ἄγρης ἐξανιών: "returning from the hunt"; < ἐξάνειμι.
δονάκων ὕπο: "on his reedpipe"; the pl. indicates that the syrinx, our Panpipe, is meant.
μοῦσαν ἀθύρων: "playing a tune."

16. παραδράμοι < παρατρέχω, here "surpass."

17. ὄρνις: the nightingale, a small thrush-like bird which often sings from cover at evening.
ἔαρος: gen. of time within which (S 1444).

18. ἐπιπροχέουσ' ἀχέει: "pouring forth (a dirge), utters." But the MSS ἐπιπροχέουσα χέει, "pouring forth, pours," should be kept. The word-play is in keeping with the style of Alexandrian hymns (e.g. Callimachus, Hymn to Apollo 25-27), and the repetition of the verb imitates the way in which a nightingale's song tumbles over itself. The poet is varying the Homeric description of the nightingale, χέει πολυηχέα φωνήν (Odyssey XIX.521).

19. σφιν: dat. sg.

20. πυκνὰ ποσσίν: not to be translated literally, "thickly with feet," but freely, "with flashing feet." The first syllable of πυκνά is short (S 145).

περιστένει: "moans around."

21. οὔρεος: with κορυφήν.

22. χορῶν: with μέσον.

23. διέπει < διέπω, "conducts"; supply χορούς as object.
λαῖφος: here, "coat," "pelt."

24. ἀγαλλόμενος: "and he takes pleasure." The circumstantial participle in this rather rambling sentence is best translated as a finite verb paralleling ἔχει.
φρένα: acc. of respect; see on VII.10.

25. τόθι: "where."

26. ἄκριτα: "unarranged," "randomly"; neuter acc. used adverbially.

28. οἷον θ': "and for example."
ἐριούνιον: See on XVIII.3.

29- The part of the nymphs' song leading up to the birth of Pan has three parts, each introduced by (ὡς) ὅ γε: how Hermes is messenger of the gods, how he came to Arcadia, and how he herded sheep for Dryops because he had fallen in love with his daughter. Note the climactic order from general to specific, least to most important.

29. ἔννεπον: "sang," imperfect; contrast ὑμνεῦσιν (present) in 27.

30. πολυπίδακα: "many-fountained."

31. οἱ . . . Κυλληνίου: "to him (in his capacity) as Cyllenian." See on XVIII.1. The gen. is used in apposition because of the idea of possession implied in the dative οἱ (S 977).

32. ψαραρότριχα: "curly-fleeced."

33. θάλε: 2nd aorist < θάλλω, "bloom," "flourish." With πόθος ὑγρός, the image is of sap rising.

34. νύμφῃ: only here with the meaning "daughter."

μιγῆναι: 2nd aorist middle infinitive < μίγνυμι; epexegetic infinitive with πόθος ὑγρός.

36. τερατωπόν: "with a marvellous face."

38. φεῦγε δ' ἀναΐξασα: "jumped up and fled," < ἀναΐσσω (Attic ἀνᾴσσω).
τιθήνη: not, as AHS suggest, his mother, but his nurse, the usual meaning of the word.

39. ἀμείλιχον: "forbidding," "harsh," explained by ἠϋγένειον, "full-bearded."

40. εἰς χε(ῖ)ρα θῆκε: "took in his arms." Ἑρμείας is nom.

41. περιώσια: "immensely"; neuter pl. acc. used adverbially.

43. πυκινοῖσιν: "close-packed, thick."
ὀρεσκῴοιο λαγωοῦ: "of a mountain-bred hare."

45. ἔτερφθεν: 3rd pl. aorist passive < τέρπω.

XX

In Homer Hephaestus, god of fire and fire's work in smithies, is son of Zeus and Hera. At Athens his cult was linked with that of Athena, the female divinity of craftsmanship, and his well-preserved temple, which contained a statue of Athena, is one of the most striking features of the area around the Agora.

3. ἐδίδαξεν: governs a double acc. of the thing and person taught.
ἐπὶ χθονός: closely with ἀνθρώπους; = ἐπιχθονίους.
τὸ πάρος: "formerly"; = πάρος.

4. ἠΰτε: "like."

5. δαέντες: aorist participle < *δάω, "learn."

6. τελεσφόρον εἰς ἐνιαυτόν: "the year around."

8. ἴληθ(ι): "be favorable"; see on I.17.

XXI

The lyre and swan were both associated with Apollo. In one myth Cycnus was a son of Apollo who, deserted by his lover, drowned himself in a lake and was transformed into a swan (κύκνος).

1. ὑπὸ πτερύγων . . . ἀείδει: "hymns you with its wings"; cf. δονάκων ὕπο XIX.5. The common mute swan of Europe has no voice, but air rushing through its flight feathers makes a clear thrumming sound.
λίγ(α): "loudly," "clearly."

2. ὄχθῃ: "on the river-bank"; dat. of place to which without a preposition.

3. Πηνειόν: the Peneus, the largest river in Thessaly.

XXII

A hymn to Poseidon, god of waters and earthquakes.

2. ἀτρυγέτοιο: See on VII.2.

3. There is some, though not much, evidence for a cult of Poseidon on Mt. Helicon, but his cult was widespread in the surrounding territory of Boeotia. Aegae, a small town in Achaea on the southern shore of the Gulf of Corinth, was known for its cult of Poseidon, as was its neighbor Helice (Iliad VIII.203).
πόντιον: "sea-god"; an adjective.

4. διχθά: adverb = δίχα, "in two," "two-fold."
τοι = σοι.
ἐδάσαντο: "allotted"; aorist < δατέομαι.

5. ἔμεναι = εἶναι and explains τιμήν.

7. πλώουσιν: "for those who sail"; dat. pl. participle < πλώω = πλέω.

XXIII

1. Ζῆνα = Δία, acc. sg. < Ζεύς.

2. εὐρύοπα < εὐρυόπης, "far-seeing."
   τελεσφόρον: "bringing things to fulfillment"; an epithet of Μοῖρα, Δίκη, the year, etc.
   Θέμιστι: In Hesiod's Theogony 900ff. Themis bears Zeus's children the Seasons, Good Order, Justice, Peace, and the Fates.

3. ἐγκλιδόν: "leaning"; adverb modifying ἑζομένη.
   οάρους ὀαρίζει: "chats chatter"; the cognate accusative (S 1564).

XXIV

To Hestia, goddess of the hearth, which was the spiritual, and in an early period the actual, center of the Greek house, as Delphi (Πυθοῖ 2) was spiritual center of the Greek world.

1. ἑκάτοιο: See on IX.1.

3. Πυθοῖ: dat. < Πυθώ, "Pytho," an old name for Delphi.
   σῶν πλοκάμων: gen. of the source. Perfumed oil was used by mortals as a hairdressing on special occasions, but the hair of the gods is perpetually anointed.

4. ἔρχεο: imperative, "come."
   τόνδ(ε) ἀνὰ οἶκον: probably the temple of Apollo at Delphi.
   θυμὸν ἔχουσα: literally, "having θυμός," i.e. "courageously." It has been questioned whether θυμός makes sense here without an epithet; see AHS.

5. ὄπασσον: "bestow," "make follow."

XXV

This hymn is a cento made of bits and pieces of Hesiod's Theogony. Lines 2-5 = Theogony 94-97 with one minor

The Shorter Homeric Hymns 37

change, 6 resembles <u>Theogony</u> 104, and the first two words of the first line recall <u>Theogony</u> 1.

2-3. ἐκ γὰρ Μουσάων . . . ἔασιν: "are from (i.e., have their origin in) the Muses"; ἔασιν = εἰσίν (S 768D). Families or guilds of rhapsodes did sometimes claim actual descent from the Muses by way of Orpheus and Homer.

4. ἐκ δὲ Διὸς βασιλῆες: The sequence of thought is somewhat clearer in Hesiod, who has been talking about the benefits that the Muses bestow on kings.

5. φίλωνται: subjunctive in a present general conditional relative clause (S 2567) without ἄν, as usually in Homer (S 2567b).

XXVI

2. Cf. VII.1.

4. κόλποισι: dat. of place where or to which without a preposition (S 1531).

5. Νύσης: See on I.8.

6. μεταρίθμιος ἀθανάτοισιν: "counted among the immortals."

8. φοιτίζεσκε: "he began to wander"; inchoative imperfect.

9. πεπυκασμένος: "made thick"; < πυκάζω.

12. ἐς ὥρας: "next year." This phrase and the following line show that this hymn was composed for some annual festival of Dionysus.

13. ἐκ δ' αὖθ' . . . ἐνιαυτούς: "and from next year for many years to come."

XXVII

Artemis, virgin huntress and mistress of wild places, leaves her mountain haunts and goes to join her brother Apollo at Delphi. In Delphic cult Artemis played a minor role, and by the end of the hymn attention has turned from Artemis alone to the divine family and attendants. The eastern pediment of the temple of Apollo at Delphi showed Apollo, Artemis, their mother Leto, and their attendants the Muses.

1. **χρυσηλάκατον** < χρυσός + ἠλακάτη, "with golden rod," usually a distaff but here referring to Artemis' bow and arrows.
   κελαδεινήν: "twanging"; modifies Ἄρτεμιν and describes the sound of Artemis' golden bow.

3. **αὐτοκασιγνήτην**: "his own sister."

5. **ἄγρῃ**: "the hunt."

6. **τρομέει**: The subject is κάρηνα, "ridges."

7. **ἔπι**: as the accent shows, adverbial with ἰαχεῖ, "cries out," "resounds."

9. **ἄλκιμον ἦτορ ἔχουσα**: "with her brave heart"; "having" is often too strong a translation for ἔχων.

10. **πάντῃ**: "everywhere," "on all sides."

11. **τερφθῇ, εὐφρήνῃ**: aorist subjunctives with ἐπήν = ἐπεὶ ἄν.

12. **νόον**: accusative of respect; see on VII.10.
    χαλάσασ(α): with ἔρχεται, "unstrings . . . and goes"; aorist participle < χαλάω.

15. **ἀρτυνέουσα** < ἀρτύνω, "order," "manage"; future participle showing purpose.

16. **παλίντονα**: "recurved."

17. **κόσμον**: "beauty."

18. **ἐξάρχουσα**: "taking the lead in"; here + acc.

ἀμβροσίην: adjective agreeing with ὄπ(α), acc. sg. of ὄψ, "voice."
ἰεῖσαι: present participle of ἵημι, "send forth." See "The Language of the Hymns," II.2.

19. ὡς τέκε: the subject of their hymn.

20. ἀθανάτων: gen. of the whole (S 1306, 1315) with ἔξοχ(α) ἀρίστους, "outstandingly best."

XXVIII

At Theogony 886-900 Hesiod tells how Zeus swallowed Metis (Intelligence), who was pregnant, and how Athena was then born from Zeus's head. This hymn adds the detail that the goddess was fully armed when she sprang out. On the similarities in language between this hymn and XXVII, see AHS.

4. μητίετα: See on I.16.

5. πολεμήϊα τεύχε(α): "warlike weapons"; cf. on XI.2.

6. παμφανόωντα: "all-gleaming"; an epic participle of παμφαίνω as though < παμφανάω.

7. πρόσθεν: "in front of."

8. ἐσσυμένως: "hastily."

9. ἐλελίζετ(ο): "spun around"; cf. I.15.

10. βρίμης: "strength," "might."
    ἀμφί: adverbial.

12. κυκώμενος < κυκάω, "stir," "mix."
    ἔσχετο: "held itself in check"; after the turmoil, the sea becomes motionless, as does the chariot of the sun (13-14).

13. Ὑπερίονος ἀγλαὸς υἱός: The Titan Hyperion was father of the sun-god Helios.

14. εἰσότε: "until."

15. εἵλετ(ο): "took (off)," an unusual meaning for the aorist middle of αἱρέω.

XXIX

See the introduction to XXIV. Hermes and Hestia were paired on the pedestal of the statue of Zeus at Olympia (Pausanias V.11,8), and there is some reason to think that the two were linked in private cult (see AHS). To explain their association in this hymn, however, is difficult and made more so by the corrupt state of the text.

2. χαμαί: locative, "on the ground"; take closely with ἐρχομένων.

3. ἀΐδιον: "everlasting," here a two-termination adjective.
πρεσβηΐδα τιμήν: "the highest honor," i.e., the portion due the eldest; πρεσβηαῖδα is < πρεσβηΐς, an alternate feminine of πρέσβυς.

5. θνητοῖσιν: dat. of advantage (S 1481); "there are no feasts for mortals."
ἵν(α): "where."
πρώτῃ πυμάτῃ τε: "first and last"; adjectives with Ἑστίῃ.

6. σπένδει: Supply τις so that οὐ (5) = οὔτις, but omit the redundant Greek negative in translating. The change of subject is harsh but understandable: "Without you there are no feasts for mortals where, beginning the libation and ending it with Hestia, anyone pours sweet wine." Even so, the text may be corrupt.

7. μοι: ethical dat. (S 1486b), almost equivalent to "please."
Ἀργειφόντα: "slayer of Argus"; voc., as is χρυσόρραπι, "with wand of gold." Hermes carries a wand, the κηρύκειον, as emblem of his function as herald.

9. ναίετε: the shift from sg. to pl. suggests that something has gone wrong with the text. Perhaps, as Allen supposes, something has dropped out of the text between lines 9 and 10. It is just possible to understand ναίετε as "construction

according to sense" (S 926a), with Hermes and Hestia implied as subjects.

10. ἐπάρηγε < ἐπαρήγω, "help."

12. ἔργματα = ἔργα.
ἔσπεσθε: aorist middle imperative of ἕπω, "attend."
ἥβῃ: "vigor"; νόῳ τε καὶ ἥβῃ is equivalent to ἥβῃ νοῦ, "mental vigor," by hendiadys (S 3025).

XXX

A hymn to Gaea, the Earth Mother.

1. παμμήτειραν: "mother of all."
ἠϋθέμεθλον: for εὐθέμεθλον, "well-founded."

2. ἐπὶ χθονί: Take with πάνθ' ὁπόσ(α) ἐστίν, "all things, however many are on earth."

3. ἠμὲν . . . ἠδ(έ): "both . . . and."

4. πωτῶνται < πωτάομαι, "fly about," frequentative of ποτάομαι = πέτομαι.
σέθεν = σοῦ.

6. πότνια: vocative.
σεῦ δ' ἔχεται: "yours it is" or "it depends on you"; the subjects are δοῦναι and ἀφελέσθαι.

7. κε = ἄν.

8. πρόφρων: "graciously"; the adjective where English would use an adverb, as also in 18.
τῷ τε: See on X.1.
ἄφθονα: "bounteous," "abundant," here predicative, "in abundance."

9. σφιν = αὐτῷ, dat. of possession.

9-10. κατ(ὰ) ἀγροὺς κτήνεσιν εὐθηνεῖ: "his fields abound in flocks"; literally, "in his fields he abounds with respect to flocks."
ἐσθλῶν: "good things"; gen. after a verb of filling (S 1369).

11. αὐτοὶ δ': "they," i.e., the men blessed by the goddess. The δέ indicates a change of subject and need not be translated here.
    κάτα: governs πόλιν, as the accent shows (S 175a).

13. εὐφροσύνῃ νεοθηλέϊ: "with fresh-blooming cheer."

14. χοροῖς φερεσανθέσιν: "with flower-laden dances."

15. παίζουσαι . . . σκαίρουσι: "skip and play"; see on XIX.24.

17. ἄλοχ(ε) Οὐρανοῦ: In Hesiod's Theogony Gaea, Earth, is the spouse of Uranus, Sky, while their daughter, the Titaness Rhea, is mother of the Olympian gods.

18. ἀντ(ι) ᾠδῆς: "in return for my song."
    βίοτον θυμήρε(α): "a pleasing life."

XXXI

This hymn and the next form a pair, one to Sun and one to Moon. They are nearly the same in length--exactly the same, if only one line has been lost after XXXI.14. Numerous similarities in language connect these two hymns and set them apart from others in the collection; the closing lines, for example, resemble no others. Few myths deal with the sun-god Helios, and his cult was well-established only on the island of Rhodes (Pindar, Olympian 7). He was, however, invoked in oaths because, as Homer says (Iliad III.277), he sees and hears everything.

1. Διὸς τέκος: refers to the Muse, since Helios, a Titan, was son of Euryphaessa and Hyperion (as in this hymn) or of Theia and Hyperion, as at Hesiod, Theogony 371-374.

2. Καλλιόπη: the chief Muse, according to Hesiod, Theogony 79. In later, Hellenistic tradition, Calliope was the muse of epic.
   βοῶπις: "ox-eyed"; an epithet frequently used of Hera and occasionally other goddesses.

4. γῆμε: unaugmented aorist of γαμέω.

ἀγακλειτήν: "glorious."

5. αὐτοκασιγνήτην: See on XXVII.3.
κάλλιμα = καλά.

6. Ἠῶ: acc. sg. of Ἠώς, "Dawn."
Σελήνην: Selene, goddess of the moon.

7. ἀκάμαντ(α): "unwearied," "tireless."

9. ἐμβεβαώς < ἐμβαίνω.
σμερδνόν = σμερδαλέον, "terribly"; neuter adjective used as adverb.

10. κόρυθος < κόρυς, "helmet."

11. αἰγλῆεν: "radiantly"; neuter adjective used as adverb.
παρὰ κροτάφων: "beside his temples."
παρειαί: "cheek-pieces" of his helmet.

12. κρατός: See on I.15.
χαρίεν: "gracefully"; neuter adjective used as adverb.

13. λάμπεται: with πνοιῇ ἀνέμων; his clothing (ἔσθος) "flickers in the blast of winds" as his chariot goes along.

14. ὑπὸ δ' ἄρσενες ἵπποι: As this incomplete phrase shows, at least one line has dropped out between 14 and 15. Perhaps the similar line endings ἵπποι and ἵππους caused a scribe's eye to skip from one to the other.

15. ἔνθ(α): refers to something in the missing line(s) preceding.

16. πέμπῃσι: perhaps anticipatory or "Homeric" subjunctive (S 1810), or the subjunctive may have been demanded by something in the missing line(s).
ὠκεανὸν δέ = Ὠκεανόνδε, "towards Ocean," the world-encircling river of Homeric geography.

18. κλήσω: "I shall glorify"; < κλείω or κλήω.
μερόπων: "speaking," "articulate."

XXXII

Selene, the moon, appears in few myths and has hardly any cult except where she is identified with other goddesses.

1. ἀείδειν: epexegetical infinitive with ἔσπετε = εἴπετε, "tell (how) to sing."
   τανυσίπτερον: "long-winged"; only here of the moon.

2. Κρονίδεω: scanned υ υ - , with -εω contracted to -ω.
   ἵστορες: "judges," literally "knowers" of song.

3. ἧς ἄπο: "from her."
   ἑλίσσεται: "rolls over," i.e., traverses. AHS suggest that γαῖαν ἑλίσσεται means "shoots to the earth" like lightning.
   οὐρανόδεικτος: "shown from heaven."

4. ὑπό: adverbial with ὄρωρεν, a reduplicated 2nd aorist < ὄρνυμι, "arise."

5. αἴγλης: gen. of the source (S 1410) with ὄρωρεν, or perhaps gen. of explanation (S 1322) defining κόσμος.
   δέ τ(ε): a combination of particles frequent in epic (GP 528); the τε need not be translated.

6. χρυσέου: scanned - υ, with synezesis and epic correption.
   ἐνδιάονται < ἐνδιάω, "linger"; the ancient grammarian Hesychius says that the middle means "to pass the zenith."

7. λοεσσαμένη = λουσαμένη, < λούω, "wash," or in the middle, "bathe."
   χρόα: acc. of respect; see on VI.14 and VII.10.

9. ἐριαύχενας: "with arching necks."

10. ἐσσυμένως προτέρωσ(ε): "hastily forwards."

11. ἑσπερίη διχόμηνος: The Greeks along with almost all other ancient Mediterranean peoples measured their months from new moon to new moon. Hence the "evening month-divider" is the full moon.
    ὅ τε: the definite article, accented because it precedes an enclitic.
    ὄγμος: "orbit."

14. τῇ = αὐτῇ, "with her"; dat. of association with a verb of, one presumes, friendly intercourse (S 1523).

15. Πανδείην: Pandeia or Pandia is an obscure figure whom ancient mythographers sometimes identified with the moon itself.

16. ἐν: "among."

18. πρόφρον: "gracious one," vocative < πρόφρων, or perhaps "graciously," if adverbial accusative.
ἐϋπλόκαμος: nom. for vocative.
κλέα < κλέος, "glory."

19. ᾄσομαι: See on VI.2.

XXXIII

See on XVII. Castor and Polydeuces were patrons of boxing, horsemanship, and, as in this hymn, seafaring.

1. ἑλικώπιδες: "with quick-glancing eyes," or perhaps "almond-eyed," a common epithet of goddesses. Cf. on VI.19.

4. ὑπό: governs κορυφῇ.

5. κελαινεφέϊ Κρονίωνι: See on XVII.4.

7. νεῶν < ναῦς, as is νηῶν in 8.
ὅτε τε: "whenever"; the τε, as often in epic, generalizes after a relative (GP 522).

8. οἱ δ': i.e., the sailors.

10. ἄρνεσσιν λευκοῖσιν: dat. of means (S 1507). White victims were appropriate to sky-gods.

10-11. ἐπ(ὶ) ἀκρωτήρια . . . πρύμνης: "onto the stern deck"; Homeric ships were undecked except for a raised platform at bow and stern.

12. (τὴν) . . . θῆκαν ὑποβρυχίην: "lay her under water"; θῆκαν is aorist in a general description (S 1932).

οἱ δ': the Dioscuri.
ἐφάνησαν: aorist passive < φαίνω.

13. ξουθῇσι: "yellow" or "tawny."

15. ἐστόρεσαν < στορέννυμι, "make level," here "calm".

16. καλὰ πόνου: "One of these words is manifestly corrupt, but the remedy has not yet been found" (AHS).

ΕΙΣ ΞΕΝΟΥΣ

Not a hymn, but found at the end of the Hymns in some manuscripts. A slightly different version is found among the so-called "Homeric epigrams," which appear in the "Herodotean" life of Homer. This composition of late antiquity says that Homer sang this epigram as he stood begging outside a cobbler's shop in Neon Teichos, near Aeolian Cyme some 28 miles north of Izmir.

1. κεχρημένον: "(one) in need of"; perfect < χράομαι.

2. πόλιν ..."Ηρης: the "steep city of Hera's lovely nymph" is Cyme.

3. πόδα νείατον: "the lowest foothill"; Saedene was a mountain in the territory of Cyme.

5. The Hermus river is the modern Gediz Cayi, which flows from "the holy mountain of the Dindymene Mother" (Herodotus I.80) to enter the sea near Foca (Phocaea) north of Izmir.